Lives & Works

Lives & Works

Interviews by

Bruce Meyer

and

Brian O'Riordan

Black Moss Press

©Bruce Meyer, Brian O'Riordan, 1992
Published by Black Moss Press
2450 Byng Rd., Windsor, Ontario
N8W 3E8.

Black Moss Books are distributed in Canada
and the United States by Firefly Books, Ltd., 250 Sparks Avenue,
Willowdale, Ontario, M2H 2S4.
All orders should be directed there.

Financial assistance toward publication of this book was gratefully
received from the Canada Council and the
Ontario Arts Council.

Cover art by Hervé Baudry

Typesetting and page design by Kristina Russelo

Canadian Cataloguing in Publication Data

Main entry under title:

Lives and works

ISBN 0-88753-223-3 (v.1)

1. Authors, Canadian — 20th century — Interviews.
I. Meyer, Bruce, 1957-   . II. O'Riordan, Brian, 1953-   .

PS8081.L58 1991   C810.9'0054   C91-090273-9
PR9186.2.L58 1991

Contents

Introduction

The interview is probably the least understood literary form in contemporary writing; it combines fiction, criticism, journalism, biography, autobiography, personal introspection, memoir, confession, propaganda and drama. The interview is a strange, indefinable hybrid, and because it reflects aspects of so many disparate elements it is a most vulnerable form of writing. The function and usefulness of a collection of interviews is further clouded when the subject for the interview is a writer. Suddenly there are new demands and expectations that enter into the picture.

With the demands placed on a book such as this, many readers expect a kind of cultural scripture to emerge — a healing, helping book, that would comfort the sick, create national unity, and solve a myriad of social and economic problems. After all, we did interview writers, and society still expects that our writers will solve our problems for us. The message, however, that came to us over and over as this book took shape was that the writer can only make suggestions, imagine possibilities, and offer criticism of those events and experiences which trouble us. A writer is not an engineer, economist, theologian, politician, or social planner. A writer can only present ideas through his or her writing, and in the end all he or she can ask is that someone should read the books, and question, interpret, and debate what emerges from the printed word.

That is the role we have taken as interviewers: as questioners, debaters, and interpreters of what we have read. This means that our approach has not been simply to ask the obvious of a writer, such as "when did you begin to write?" or "how long does it take you to write this or that?" but to read the writer's works from a critical perspective — to present that perspective to the writer, and to listen intently to the response in search of further questions. What few readers of the contemporary literary interview realise is that the interviewers must be critics. The interviewers must approach a subject with an earnest desire to illuminate the text with whatever explicatory material the writer has to offer. Sometimes the response on the author's part takes the form of biographical background; sometimes the author responds by re-examining our stance and offering a completely unexpected view — the personal view — of a certain work. In other instances, a question and answer can lead to larger issues.

What the interviewers must do throughout the interview process is remain alert to possibilities. The writer's process is the exploration and divination of the unseen and the unexpected (at least that is what they tell you). A background in practical criticism and a thorough knowledge of the life and the work of an author is an essential ingredient in a successful interview. The relationship between the author and the interviewer, therefore, is very akin to the relationship between the author and the critic. It is a circumstance of living and learning.

The literary interview, however, dwells in the strange, and still undefined grey area between primary and secondary text, the same area in which scholars find letters, apologias, and marginal notes which enhance, and at the same time limit, the readings of a text. The problem is this: should a reader read secondary material such as letters, marginalia, or interviews? The answer is a matter of taste, depth, and interest. Surely a thorough scholar will wish to know as much about a certain work as he or she can, especially when such information issues from the author. Herein lies another problem.

The interview, of course, may be a red herring in the critical process. What an author has to say about a given work is certainly not the final word. The situation is complicated further by the fact that the interview is partly a fiction in that the writers portray themselves not only as they are and as we encounter them but as they wish to be depicted. They are conscious of the image they are allowing to come between themselves and their works. The interview is a kind of a pose — like the self-conscious gesturing contained in a rock video. It is supposed to underline the meaning of the lyrics, but also mischievously such media can subvert them; it is all in the ear and the eye of the beholder.

What we have discovered in the process of compiling this book, however, is that nothing exists in a vacuum. A member of the school of New Criticism (which, ironically, is now old criticism), would argue that biography has absolutely no place in a critical response, and that the text is a pristine work of art always free from distracting pressures and influences. The times, his/her companions and literary associations, his/her family, and often his/her immediate circumstances and beliefs, come to bear on a work of literature so that the work itself cannot even exist within the vacuum of the author's creative process. To this effect, we decided to title this book *Lives and Works* because the two seemed inseparable. The authors themselves showed an uncanny desire to set certain ideas straight, to tidy up after the fact, and often after the critics; to defend their ideas, and their words; to reshape the works in the image of their intent; and to salvage their version of the artificial act from the absurdities of misreadings. The interview is almost a literary post-script to the text where the author assumes the role of self-critic, editor, and reinventor (to say nothing of propagandist) to save the work from its critics — a reversal of the old chestnut about the critic saving the work from the author. Ironically, what the interview form often creates is a portrait of the artist as a third person.

Our role as interviewers has been to maintain an even balance, as much as possible, between the apparent work which emerges from our reading, and the recreated work which often emerges from the author's viewpoint, and to keep ourselves as objective as we possibly can in the process. A number of readers of *In Their Words* questioned why two interviewers should not be identified by their individual names. From our point of view, what is important is the question and not the questioner. The label, "*Interviewers*," allows us a kind of distance and keeps us from getting in the way of the author. The same people referred to us simply as "editors."

The interviewer is not an editor. The interviewer is part researcher, scholar, critic, journalist, historian, detective, and above all a writer. The interviewer as a writer is revealed when the interview is considered to be a form of chronicle. A good interview strives to be faithful to the author's words — we have allowed our subjects to check their typescripts for accuracy, phrasing, and expression — because the finished product is a form of verbal literary history in which an interplay takes place between the life and the works of an author, and between the works, the author, and the presence of critical interpretation. The unsuccessful interview promotes only the author's personality, reveals little of the creative process of a written work, limits its scope to a certain work, cause, or idea, or simply trivializes itself to the level of publisher's propaganda.

The "star" status which has been accorded to writers in this century stems not only from the Shelleyan concept of the writer as social legislator, but from the premise that the writer is the keeper of mystery, and oracular puzzles. Granted, writers love causes, especially when their craft and gift — articulation — can play an active role in persuading people to change their attitudes and ideas; but what becomes evident from these interviews is that there is no mystery to problem solving. The message that was made clear to us was that a writer communicates, that a writer wishes to share his or her dreams, ideas, and concerns with anyone who will listen — even the readers of interviews — and that this process of sharing is, in fact, a kind of generosity and catharsis of spirit. What we have attempted to show in this book is the process of the creative spirit behind the public or literary persona; and the process of minds revealing themselves in the process of revealing their own creative methods and desires.

Canada has, in recent years, become a nation of dialogue, of open forums, and debates, a place where national anxieties and objections have been aired for all to hear. Under this regime of dialogue, the interview format has flourished. Everyone seems to have an opinion, and, perhaps to our relief and as a reflection of our civilised attitude toward our problems, there is still the desire to hear what others have to say. The reason why people are drawn to the interview form stems from a mixture of desires: to be enlightened; to eavesdrop on an interesting conversation; and to participate in a miniature drama, as in either the role of the interviewer or the author. The typescript style, where the conversant is identified by name, is the style in which most dramas find their printed form. Each piece in this collection is dependent on this interaction between individuals. Each interview opens with a scene being set, with background information on the author, and the place and time of the interview. What follows is an event where time and place are momentarily suspended — a dramatic fiction (if one wishes to read it in that way), and an exchange of ideas.

The very nature of the interview hinges upon the success or failure of transcribed and edited conversation, and some subjects are simply better conversationalists than others. Therefore, the interview appears to be better. In one case, where a subject muttered through one of our two hour exchanges and displayed a range of disconcerting body language, we left the venue with the feeling that we had failed. Later, we discovered, as we transcribed the tape, that the answers to our questions had more depth, emotion, and substance than we had imagined. Detached and after the fact as the interview form appears, it allows the interviewees — in this case fourteen writers — the opportunity to focus their attention on what they were saying — and that, after all, is one of the goals of writing.

Needless to say, the interview is a demanding form to work with. What complicates matters further is the fact that these subjects are not only writers but Canadian writers. With the current national political situation, its uncertainties, and pressures lurking in the background of just about any text in the contemporary Canadian literary milieu, it is a wonder that anything coherent, anything resembling a thread of continuity emerges from the pages of this book. Yet there are several threads that bear recognition.

There is a terrible pressure on Canadian writers to be political — political in the broad sense of the term. Such pressures include the national unity debate, the language question, the issues of the environment, gender and equity, regional representation, religious differences, multiculturalism, and global stability. The Canadian writer is faced with the problem of having to satisfy these 'political' demands in order to remain relevant to a constantly distracted and diminishing issue-oriented readership. And what is the problem for the writer reflects what has become a problem for the nation. The dilemma facing the country and its writers is that Canada is trying to be all things to all people. The broad definition of what a Canadian is or should be has been lost in the shuffle of secondary concerns and debates, has been blurred beyond recognition and stretched out of shape to the point that the anxieties we are experiencing as a nation stem from an inability to see ourselves in the total picture. The miraculous aspect that emerges from our conversations with these writers, however, is that our writers do have a vision of the country, a vision which locates us not only in the national context but in the broader context of human nature, experience, and endeavour; the imperative that we discover and apply our imaginations and our own experiences to the process of problem solving. What is surprising is that during the recent constitutional debate, Canadians listened to the politicians and a repeated series of political clichés — yet we did not listen to our writers although they have been and remain the better counsels of our collective conscience. The writer not only locates us in our experience; he or she fills in the details and frames the situation within the limits of recognisable experience. Too often, though, we view writers as background noise, or fail to see the culture for the cultural rhetoric and apparatus.

Such was the case with the great cultural debate about "identity" that emerged from the Centennial celebrations. The need to find writers and to create an instant literature superseded the content of the literature — we missed a valuable opportunity to listen to what writers had to say because of the urgency with which we required that they make their statements. During the Seventies and the Eighties, a kind of cultural complacency overtook Canada, in particular English Canada, and it became fashionable to dismiss the "identity" debate because such dialogue was viewed suspiciously as an allusion to an absence of culture, an anxiety bordering on mass insecurity. Doggedly, the writers kept writing.

The issue now is no longer one of identity but of nationality; and by nationality we embrace the term both in the cultural and the political sense of the word. The question now is not "do we have a literature?"

or the strange geographical and social solipsism of "where is here?" The question that confronts both Canadian writers and readers of 1992 is whether we wish to see Canada remain an integrated sum of all its disparate parts, or whether we wish to see it become a series of parts alluding vaguely to a disparate sum.

Lives and Works, by accident rather than by design, has an equal number of men and women, and regional representation from most parts of the country: Rooke from the West Coast; Mouré, Bissoondath and Jones from Quebec; Crozier, Wiseman, Lane and Newlove from the Prairies; Atwood, Avison, Wallace and Kogawa from Ontario; and MacLeod from the Maritimes.

There is only so much room in a book — and we intend to continue a process that we began in 1985 with *In Their Words* (that book included Irving Layton, Leonard Cohen, Timothy Findley, Dorothy Livesay, Eli Mandel, Gwendolyn MacEwen, Milton Acorn, Brian Moore, Roo Borson, Sheila Watson, Raymond Souster, Elizabeth Smart, James Reaney, and Al Purdy). Our goal is to create a conversational chronicle, not only of our literature and its writers, but of the national ethos that those writers articulate as it develops and evolves over a long period. Our aim is not regional balance but national overview; to find what is Canadian in the broad experience, and to provide a forum for those voices that would articulate such a notion.

The tidy parcelling of authors into regional classifications is a rather pointless exercise which satisfies critical concerns but is, in reality, the least of many concerns in the minds of those authors we have interviewed. From the perspectives of these authors as they communicated them to us, being a human being and a writer, and perhaps being a Canadian writer, far outstrips the notions of regional "identity" which often emerge from a misreading of the use of setting. To the writer, especially the Canadian writer, a work of literature is not set in a place as much as it is set in their own imagination. Perhaps the nationality this country seeks has already been created and is simply waiting to be discovered in the works of its authors.

We hope that through these interviews readers will discover a Canadian consciousness and awareness that transcends many of the current and future political debates about our identity, our destination, our beliefs, ideas, languages, and assumptions. Our writers and their imaginations, their lives and their works, are not our only natural resource, but they are key to unlocking the future. Canada, after all, is more a psychological construct than a political or geographical space: it is an outlook, a form of perception, a wild creation of the imagination which embodies a myriad of landscapes, ideas, assumptions, languages, beliefs, and histories. All that remains is to allow the writers to articulate that vision to readers who are longing to believe, once again, in the validity and security of the Canadian experience.

Bruce Meyer & Brian O'Riordan
Toronto, December 4, 1991

Acknowledgements

The Interviewers wish to thank the following individuals for their assistance in the preparation of this book: the fourteen writers who generously gave of their time, their ideas, and their hospitality; Marty Gervais and Kris Russelo of Black Moss Press; Homer Meyer and Margaret Meyer; Brian's wife, Rina Colaiacovo; Dr. Carolyn Meyer; Bev Daurio; Zulfikar Ghose and Christopher Middleton of Austin, Texas; Mark Kingwell; Ted Plantos; Robert Stacey; Adina Sarig of Adina Photo, Toronto; the staff of the Auberge Hatley Inn, North Hatley, Quebec. Also, many thanks to the Ontario Arts Council, The Writers' Union of Canada, The League of Canadian Poets, Playwrights Canada, and the Lucinda Vardey Literary Agency.

Some of these interviews have appeared previously in *Poetry Canada Review*, *Northward Journal*, *Cross Canada Writers' Quarterly*, *Acta Victoriana*, and *The University of Toronto Review*.

B.M.
B. O'R.

Figure It Out:

Margaret Atwood

What can be said about Margaret Atwood that has not been said before? What has she herself said that she has not said before? Has anyone been listening to what she has said or have they simply heard from her what they wanted to hear, and written about her accordingly? Inevitably, in speaking with Margaret Atwood there is the temptation to speak to and about her mythical selves rather than the mythos which she is addressing in her own writing and extra literary concerns. Nominated in recent years for both the Nobel Prize and the Booker Prize, Atwood is arguably one of the best novelists in the English language, and one of the most widely read contemporary writers.

On a hot June day in the Annex area of Toronto we arrived on Atwood's doorstep. She had recently returned from delivering the Clarendon Lectures at Oxford University, and was preparing to depart for Iceland and France. We sat down around a circular, lace-covered parlour table in a corner of her white living room. A small cat jumped into her lap and she sat stroking its fur calmly throughout the interview.

Conversation with Margaret Atwood is like a game. She listens intently, and hones in on every word, correcting, detecting the false note in both herself and in our questions. She is not deserving of her reputation as a tough interview subject. She likes accuracy and precision of thought and language — in effect, what she says is an extension of her writing, and she is very conscious of her role not only as a literary voice, but as a public persona and spokesperson for a host of causes. She does not take herself lightly or for granted, yet at the same time she is charming, witty, and insightful. She approaches an interview as she would any other literary form — with exacting standards and an eye to the rules, whatever they may be.

Margaret Atwood was born in Ottawa in 1939, and spent extensive periods of her childhood in Northern Ontario and Quebec.

She was educated at Victoria College, University of Toronto, and Radcliffe College, Harvard. Her works of poetry include *Double Persephone* (1961), *The Circle Game* (1966, for which she won the Governor General's Award), *The Animals in that Country* (1968), *The Journals of Susanna Moodie* (1970), *Procedures for Underground* (1970), *Power Politics* (1973), *You Are Happy* (1974), *Selected Poems* (1976, 1986, 1990), *Two Headed Poems* (1978), *True Stories* (1981), *Murder in the Dark* (1983), and *Interlunar* (1984). Her novels are *The Edible Woman* (1969), *Surfacing* (1972), *Lady Oracle* (1976), *Life Before Man* (1979), *Bodily Harm* (1981), *The Handmaid's Tale* (1985, for which she won the Governor General's Award), *Cat's Eye* (1988); and her short story collections are *Dancing Girls* (1977), *Bluebeard's Egg* (1983) and *Wilderness Tips* (1991). She has also written *Survival: A Thematic Guide to Canadian Literature* (1972), and *Second Words*, a collection of her critical writings (1982). She lives in Toronto with writer Graeme Gibson and their daughter. This interview was conducted on June 6, 1991.

Interviewers: Is there one myth or particular misreading about your writing that you wish could be corrected?

Atwood: Myths tend to explode themselves. The horrible secret is, I don't read a lot of critical writing about my work. There is so much, I would be driven mad if I did. If you had asked me that question in, say, 1973 or 1974, it would have been a lot easier to answer because there was a lot less written. At that time, people were very struck by the fact that a female writer was writing books that had tough things in them. But this is no longer true: many women writers have gone into those territories. For a while, I was getting, "Her stuff is very bleak, dark, and negative." Then people figured out it was funny, and they

said, "Gee, she's really funny." As with any writer, people look up the previous criticism and then write something to contradict it, because that's the only way they can make an impact. They say, "The others had it all wrong. I am now going to reveal the real truth." They must overturn, you see, the previously-held view.

Interviewers: They never knock you off stride, though?

Atwood: Well, there's nothing anybody could possibly say that hasn't already been said. But some things are going to be recycled because there are only so many versions of a person you can come up with. I've had Medusa. I've had the Virgin Mary. You wouldn't believe the stuff that started coming out when I had a baby.

Interviewers: Margaret the Mother?

Atwood: Yes. Suddenly, they wanted to see me as warm and motherly. I was still the same person, but they used a different iconography. I've been accused of hating women. I've been accused of hating men. I've been accused of not hating either of them enough. (Laughter). Getting too soft on everybody. I've been accused of being ideological; of not being ideological enough. You can make it up with filing cards: write down everything you can think of, and then write down the opposite of everything you've written. And there you have it. You could do a fun calendar to promote some worthy cause, using excerpts from critics who mutually contradict one another.

Interviewers: Like a kaleidoscope image where they keep turning it around to get different patterns of the same picture?

Atwood: Maybe it's good, because it means there's enough in your work to support many different analyses. How much can you write about something one-dimensional? The real drawback is that at a certain point you, as a person, and your work, get condensed into something else; you become like the word *socialism*, or *fascism* — everybody is now supposed to know what that reference means. You become one of those "idea chips" that people move around.

Interviewers: You recently gave the Clarendon Lectures at Oxford.

Atwood: Yes. That was lots of fun. I enjoyed that.

Interviewers: In the first lecture, published in Books in Canada, *one of the authors you wrote about was Robert Service. You noted that most serious critics usually dismiss him.*

Atwood: His work is the motherlode of Northern imagery.

Interviewers: You went on to say, in that lecture, "To sum up: popular lore, and popular literature, established early that the North was uncanny, awe-inspiring in an almost religious way, hostile to white men, but alluring; that it would lead you on and do you in; that it would drive you crazy and, finally, claim you for its own."

Atwood: That's certainly Service's version of the North. There were four Clarendon Lectures. Three of them were on different groups of images associated with the North. The first one was, basically, the Frozen Explorer group, in which the North is represented by a group of female images which you can trace from Service right through Pratt and Gwendolyn MacEwen. The second lecture was on people who wanted to turn themselves into Indians.

Interviewers: Like Earnest Thompson Seton, Grey Owl, or Frank Prewett?

Atwood: Yes, and how that carried through into other works such as Robert Kroetsch's novel *Gone Indian*, in which the hero is a person who wants to imitate Grey Owl. He doesn't want to imitate an Indian; he wants to imitate a white man who wanted to imitate an Indian, which is a different thing. The third one was on Wendigos. The fourth one was on how the imagery changes when the literature is written by women. The odd thing is that when women write literature in which the protagonists are male, things stay very much the same. When, however, women writers write pieces in which the protagonist is female, things change.

Interviewers: In what way?

Atwood: The Service complex, in which the North is mean and female, changes. When you change the protagonist from a man to a woman, as in Ethel Wilson's *Swamp Angel*, Nature does not have a gender. But when the protagonist is male, as in that classic story, "The Old Woman," by Joyce Marshall, the complex image, "mean/north/female," is very close to Service's. Gwendolyn MacEwen has this icy virgin as well. When the protagonist is male (and the problem with explorers is that none of them were female in the Canadian North, and if you made up a poem about one it would obviously be an ironic fantasy—Jane Franklin meets Mrs. Rasmussen), the landscape ends up driving the guy nuts, as is the case in Joyce Marshall's story. Nature, in that instance, is very obviously female. The writer is a woman, but the protagonist is a man. However, when the protagonist is a woman, what are your choices? You could have a mean female Nature if you wanted to, but what relation would she bear to the female protagonist? Would she be a mother? An evil sister? A wicked step-mother? A lesbian lover? Usually, the women writers using female protagonists don't give Nature a gender. In these cases, Nature is more often viewed as a place in which to seek refuge rather than something that will destroy you. In Marian Engels' *Bear*, for instance, the bear is male, but the natural world surrounding it is gender-neutral. It is not Mother Nature.

Interviewers: Pratt's iceberg in "The Titanic" for instance…

Atwood: Is female. Just before he started work on "The Titanic," Pratt was working on a poem about the Franklin Expedition, and the only reason he didn't write that poem was that he couldn't get up there to see the terrain at first-hand.

Interviewers: One of the recurring themes in literature about the north, as you point out in the first lecture, is that of submergence. You mention MacEwen's passages about Franklin's ships Erebus *and* Terror, *and she has them sink. Klein's "A Portrait of the Poet as a Landscape" is another work of 'submergence' that comes to mind.*

Atwood: Everyone seems to want to get those dead people under the water. (Laughter).

Interviewers: Why?

Atwood: I don't know. Some of my speculation centres around the fact that the Victorians, in general, were very fascinated by drowned people.

Interviewers: Arthur Henry Hallam of Tennyson's "In Memoriam?"

Atwood: That's the one I mentioned in my lecture, but he's not the only one.

Interviewers: An echo of Milton's "Lycidas," perhaps?

Atwood: Who knows? Could be. Victorian English poetry is keen on drowned people.

What we may have been doing as Canadians was borrowing the drowned people, although we have a lot of water and many people do drown in it. There are quite a few drowned people in Ethel Wilson's works, by the way.

Interviewers: Is it because we have a craving, in our literature, for an unattainable pastoral vision? "Lycidas" is, after all, a pastoral poem.

Atwood: It may all go back to Shakespeare.

Interviewers: To The Tempest?

Atwood: Yes. Drowning seems a more poetic way of dying than sticking your fork into an electrical outlet. There are a lot of literary associations with drowning.

Interviewers: And the artistic associations in the Canadian context, such as the death of Tom Thompson.

Atwood: Yes, but he was just "falling into" an established mode. He became part of the tradition of the female North claiming those whom she loves, taking you unto herself; the tradition of the drowned artist, the drowned lyrical person. Let's just say that drowning, and to a certain extent freezing, are more literary ways of dying than car crashes.

Interviewers: Except in the case of Albert Camus?

Atwood: (Laughter). Or breaking your neck by falling down the stairs. Many people die that way, but we don't have lyrical poems about them; we don't have any mythology about the goddess of the cellar stairs taking you unto herself. You're just as dead, but there aren't the same associations.

Interviewers: The North has those associations of danger. In an article you wrote for Saturday Night, *"True North," in 1987, you said that the*

North "focuses our anxieties." What are those anxieties?

Atwood: Let me just say that in any country, there are a couple of key words that will cause people to lean forward in their chairs and start telling you stories. You can test this out if you go to Australia and say the words 'Outback' or 'sharks.' You'll immediately hear a number of stories about people who encountered sharks and escaped them, people who knew other people who encountered sharks and did not escape them, people who got lost in the Outback, and people who knew other people who got lost in the Outback, even though most Australians live in cities, never encounter a shark, and never get lost in the Outback. Those are very potent words for them. Those are the words that focus their anxieties, even though they are much more likely to die in a car crash.

For us, it's getting lost in the bush, drowning, freezing to death, and bears. Of these four things, "bears" is the most universal fear. Coast to coast. Bears are an imaginative possibility, even though they might not be a real possibility.

We do many more dangerous things every day than getting lost in the bush; and maybe we should refocus our anxieties. If we really were aware of what it might involve to get into a car and drive, we probably wouldn't do it. But the notion of a large, dangerous animal still haunts us.

Interviewers: Isn't there a discrepancy between the way Canadians live their day-to-day lives in southern cities and the way they imagine themselves through the concept of North?

Atwood: Just as there is a discrepancy between what English people experience in their day-to-day lives and the ideas of castles, the Tower of London and Shakespeare's Stratford-on-Avon. They are not living that life anymore. But it remains part of the imaginative world.

Interviewers: And our discrepancies are things like the Franklin Expedition?

Atwood: Yes. Those symbols still exist, and act as orientation points.

Interviewers: Do readers buy that because literature is a means of escaping to something different?

Atwood: It depends what you're being asked to buy. If you are reading Mordecai Richler's *Solomon Gursky,* and you come across the parody of the Franklin Expedition, it helps to know something about the primary material.

Interviewers: Throughout your work, you've touched on the theme of the tension between the creator and the creation. In "Speeches for Dr. Frankenstein," in Lady Oracle *— where you have a writer writing a novel — and in* Cat's Eye, *where Elaine Risley is trying to deal with her own past through her paintings, you touch on this.*

Atwood: That's interesting. I don't think about that a lot myself. I'm not a preacher. I'm not a politician. I'm not "developing themes." I'm telling stories. I'm rendering material.

Interviewers: Sometimes, in fact, you rework that material, rework situations, as is the case with Marlene in Lady Oracle, *who seems to be a precursor of Cordelia in* Cat's Eye.

Atwood: In *Lady Oracle,* though, that's the sideshow. In *Cat's Eye,* it's the seminal incident. The harassment of Elaine by Cordelia, and the subsequent fallout, is the subject of the book. That book is about nasty relationships among little girls, which have not been treated very much in fiction for adults. In *Lady Oracle* it's done as a comic turn, much as it is in *Anne of Green Gables* with Josie Pye, and much as it is with many of those Enid Blyton schoolgirl novels in which the bad little girls are ultimately deflated and conquered. In *Anne of Green Gables* you have Diana, who is always good, and Josie Pye, who is always bad. In reality, they were probably the same person, sometimes good, sometimes bad. No one is all good or all bad.

But bad little boys are bad in different ways. Little boys have much more stable hierarchies than little girls do. The reason for the leader of the little boys being the leader is very obvious. He's the best at baseball, or he's got the best collection of baseball cards. He's good at something, and you can see what he's good at. The hierarchy does not change unless the reasons for the establishment of the hierarchy change. With girls, there's no obvious reason for the top girl being on top. Because of this, the opportunities for girls to be more manipulative and conspiratorial and Machiavellian are greater, and conspiracies to overthrow the top girl are much more possible. There is a lot less physicality among little girls. Little boys fight, but don't hold grudges. Girls are more verbal, and more subtle. Little girls have an overt dislike of out and out confrontation; they'll whisper and exclude rather than fight.

The early mythology of the Women's Movement — that women were born into sisterhood — is no more true than to say that women are born into motherhood. The styles of motherhood are very much learned, as are the styles of relationships among women.

Interviewers: There is a strong sense of inquiry in your approach to your material, whether fiction or non-fiction.

Atwood: Surely that's at the root of all writing. I'm interested in exploring the consequences of situations.

Interviewers: Do you, therefore, write with a view to what the ending will be?

Atwood: No. The ending emerges.

Interviewers: You satirise the whole notion of endings in "Happy Endings," in Murder In the Dark.

Atwood: When you read Part A out loud, people burst into spontaneous laughter and cheers. Why is that? It's because everyone knows how they want to live, but they know life isn't like that. They know nobody's life goes that smoothly. Everyone wants to be happy. But it's not so easy.

Interviewers: You wrote in "Writing the Male Character" that as a writer you wanted the "Cloak of Invisibility and the ability to teleport your mind into somebody else's while still retaining your own perceptions and memory."

Atwood: I'd settle for a telephone tap. (Laughter).

Interviewers: And you went on to say "these two fantasies are what novelists act out every time they write." This seems to suggest, as you write in Cat's Eye, *that you almost have to exist in two places at once in order to write. There's a sense of working out a personal nostalgia for a time and place.*

Atwood: *Cat's Eye* is not based on "personal nostalgia;" it's a rendering of a time. According to the mail I received, it's not very "personal" at all, because almost everyone who has written to me has indicated that he or she has gone through some of the experiences I write about in *Cat's Eye*. Some of them send me samples of their marble collection. (Laughter). But real marbles aside, I do realise that the marble is the structural element in the book. The marble is to *Cat's Eye* as the *madelaine* is to Proust. It's a very nice structural element, because marbles go back at least to ancient Egypt as divination objects. They were used for telling the future.

Interviewers: At the beginning of Cat's Eye you quote Stephen Hawking, the English physicist:

"Why do we remember the past and not the future?"

Atwood: Hawking was one of the seven or eight of those kinds of guys I was reading at the time. I also have a nephew who sets me straight on matters relating to physics. But Hawking writes so well.

Interviewers: *It is unusual to have scientists as characters in novels, as you do in* Life Before Man *and* Cat's Eye.

Atwood: This is because most novelists don't know enough about science, or it just wouldn't occur to them. Their characters are more likely to be journalists, university professors, somebody within their reach. My scientists are not gothic scientists. They're not evil, like Dr. Moreau.

Interviewers: *But you had a background in science.*

Atwood: Exactly. My father was an entomologist. My brother is a neurophysiologist. I have some cousins who are doctors. I have a relative who is an atomic metallurgist. I did science myself, and almost became a biologist.

Interviewers: *It seems à propos to blend science and fiction because they both seek explanations.*

Atwood: Maybe. Then, of course, there's science fiction, which is hard to write well. You can't cheat on the facts or get sloppy, because you'll get called on the floor right away; the scientists will catch you out. You can't write Buck Rogers stuff anymore.

Interviewers: *You have dabbled on the fringes of science fiction in* The Handmaid's Tale *and in your short story written after that: "Freeforall."*

Atwood: Which is another extrapolation —

like *The Handmaid's Tale* — from the present situation in the world.

Interviewers: *The situation in the story seems to be reversed from that in the novel. The males are now the handmaids...*

Atwood: Figure it out. If AIDS, a sexually transmitted disease, is the big plague, that's how things would be, because you can tell whether a woman is a virgin or not, but you can't tell whether a male is. *Lock them up,* some would say: it's the only way! If you want uncontaminated marriages, that's what you're going to have to do. You're going to have to lock up the male children before you marry them off.

Interviewers: *The story is the flip-side of* The Handmaid's Tale. *Are you saying anything is possible in a totalitarian regime?*

Atwood: Any twist in human life is possible if there is somebody with absolute control. We have seen all the elements of this in our own time. I didn't invent anything in either story. Both are based on actuality or possibility. They aren't science fiction of the green monster variety, they're speculative fiction of the George Orwell variety.

Interviewers: *In the "Epilogue" to* The Handmaid's Tale, *besides obviously being able to use it to send up standard academic analysis...*

Atwood: What's to send up? It sends itself up.

Interviewers: *The "Epilogue" certainly provides a much different conclusion to the work than what is offered by the ending of the film version of* The Handmaid's Tale.

Atwood: Films are a different medium. Films are short, and they're made with images, not words; they can only handle two or three levels of meaning; they can only handle two or three levels of time; they can't handle metaphor; and everything in them is very literal and visible. If the film makers had kept the Epilogue, suddenly at the end of the film there would have been a whole new set of characters you'd never seen before. The audience would have said, "What's going on?" The problems they had were the problems of film. The other problem with film is the problem of internal monologue. They were planning on using a voice-over narration, but that disappeared in the process.

Film starts. It goes at the pace at which it goes. It's like an airline trip — you're buckled in. But with a book, if there's something you didn't get, you can turn back and re-read it, slow it down. A book is much more malleable in the hands of a reader than a film is in the eyes of a viewer. A viewer can't stop the film or slow it down (unless you're using a VCR). The book, to me, is a much more democratic form, even though film is a larger mass media. The viewer of a film is more manipulated by it — more controlled by it — than a reader is controlled by a book. In order to read a book, the readers must use their imaginations. They fill in, they help create the scenes and the characters. The characters in a film look like the actors, not like your idea of the characters. Films create very definite images which are powerful but monolithic.

Also, books are a lot easier to produce than films, in that they are cheaper to make. Publishing books is something else again, although still a lot less expensive than films. If you write for film, unless you are very very stupid, you learn early on that films are not a writer's medium. You're not in control of the process. Scenes get carved up, taken out, end up on the cutting room floor.

Interviewers: *You have a fascination with "Middle Kingdoms," in your works, places that stand between extremes, or are in themselves in transition from one extreme to another. Gilead, for example, in* The Handmaid's Tale. *Even the Arctic is a kind of a middle kingdom.*

Atwood: A strange land between heaven and hell, as Service has it.

Interviewers: *Frye used to point out that Canada was in that situation politically between the U.S.S.R. and the U.S.A. On the subject of politics, during the Free Trade debate you told the apocryphal story, in front of the Commons Committee on International Trade, of how beavers, when frightened, chew off their own balls and offer them to their enemies. You seemed to be saying that this was what Canada was doing by agreeing to free trade with the U.S.*

Atwood: That metaphor certainly got a lot of those guys upset.

Interviewers: *Did they see themselves as beavers?*

Atwood: No. They saw themselves as threatened. (Laughter). They saw their sexual prowess as having been called into question. That sentence got quoted a lot, with great indignation.

Interviewers: *You wrote in the poem, "Notes Toward A Poem That Can Never Be Written," "in this country you can say what you like because no one will listen to you anyway." Was that the case for you during the Free Trade Debate?*

Atwood: Well, the reality is that those of us opposed to the deal did not have four million dollars to throw around during the last two weeks of the campaign.

But these are not things I do as a writer. These are things I do as a citizen. Writers end up saying things like this because most other people would be fired for saying them.

Conversion
and
Meditation:

Margaret Avison

In the first issue of *The Tamarack Review*, Margaret Avison wrote that "A poem is an event. Only in sequence, and in retrospect, can the full import of an event be assessed." In every poet's career, however, there is that vantage point from which he or she can stand back and see all the events in their sequence and perceive some order or pattern in the way they have taken their course. Margaret Avison continues to meditate on many events, especially her conversion to Christianity, a conversion which changed her life absolutely and dramatically.

We met her in the small sunlit office of the Mustard Seed Mission in Forest Hill Village, Toronto. The window faced onto hydro wires that were strung from an ice-covered telephone pole. As we took off our coats, Avison talked enthusiastically about the mission's educational work in Taiwan and Papua New Guinea, and she cleared a place on her cluttered desk for tea and sandwiches.

Born in Galt, Ontario in 1918, she grew up in Western Canada before returning to Ontario to attend Victoria College where she studied English under poet E.J. Pratt and novelist J.D. Robbins. She has worked as a librarian, a social worker, an archivist and a lecturer. Her first collection of poetry, *Winter Sun* (1960) won the Governor General's Award for Poetry. This was followed by *The Dumbfounding* (1966), *Sunblue* (1978), *No Time* (1989), *Selected Poems* (1991), and a second Governor General's Award for Poetry. In January of 1985, shortly before we spoke with her, she was awarded the Order of Canada.

Interviewers: *Christianity is one of the major concerns of your work. Did this concern, this preoccupation develop from a religious upbringing?*

Avison: My father was a Methodist minister who deeply respected the printed page. He went out to the prairies at the tail-end of the fake-evangelical movement. I remember one revivalist meeting where everyone who was to be 'saved' was asked to stand. Everyone stood except for this girl I knew in the choir called Kate Brown. She was our family hero for doing that. (Laughter). My father was a very warm, very imaginative man. He had grown up as a foster child. His marital home was the only real home he'd ever known. My mother built up his confidence, but I think as a young man he was a little melancholy. But he was very happy in his older years. He followed the CCF with great interest. During the War he headed up the protests over what was happening to the Nissei, the forced displacement of Japanese-Canadians away from the British Columbia coast to the interior of Alberta. There were masses of work done in Ottawa about this but it all fizzled away.

Interviewers: Where in the West was your father's congregation?

Avison: The Methodist Church system worked on the basis of three-year placements. He was scattered around the West and before that in Ontario. When I was two, he was sent to Regina and when I was six, he went on to Calgary. He was there when the United Church Union of 1928 took place.

Interviewers: It must have been a great transition for you, coming east to Toronto in the late Thirties to study at Victoria College.

Avison: Not as much of a transition as you might think. My father had already been moved back here before I enrolled at university. But it did have a disastrous impact on me after living in Alberta. I had a long drawn-out homesickness. The West was all I knew. It was a very happy time for me. I was hopeful upon entering college because I hadn't liked high-school and hoped university would be different. I remember that during my first term at the University of Toronto I went to the old library, which is now the Science and Medicine Library, and looked up in the card index anything written before the sixteenth century. I did that just because this was university and that was the sort of thing you should be able to find in a university library.

Interviewers: You worked on the college magazine, Acta Victoriana, *as have many other aspiring young authors in their college days — Atwood, Lee, Frye, Pratt. Did working on* Acta Victoriana *get you started on writing poetry?*

Avison: No. My first published poem was in the *Calgary Herald* while I was still out West. I was about eight. It was at that point, I guess, that I decided that I was a writer. Or, at least, the family decided it for me. They put the idea in my head.

Interviewers: What was the first poem about?

Avison: It was something about taking a sled out in the winter in the snow and sliding downhill. I started writing seriously, though, when I got to high-school.

Interviewers: Was there any particular person, at that time, who encouraged you?

Avison: Yes. My grade-nine teacher, Gladys Storey. She had a poetry club that met after school. She would ask us all to bring some work and would collect it anonymously. At one session she said: "Would the person who wrote 'Ode to an Apple Core' remain behind." That was me! She read everything I gave her and her criticisms were good.

Interviewers: Was there any particular comment she made that stood out?

Avison: Yes. I will always remember something she wrote in red ink in one of my notebooks: "It is easy to be profound and gloomy or to be superficial and happy but the achievement will be when you are able to be profound and happy." She told me to never write a poem with a first-person pronoun in it until I had finished high-school. That was a tremendous piece of wisdom. It turns you from the personal without really telling you to do that. Then she did the final clever thing for me of dying at the end of my grade-nine year. It wasn't just my feeling of grief that was so memorable, that made her such an influence. During a service for the whole school, I remember vividly, eight grade thirteen boys fainted and were carried out. It was like ballad poetry with the knights on their biers.

Interviewers: Were there any other significant early influences or mentors for you in your work?

Avison: As a device for having a holiday in the United States I did a wonderful course on Hardy with the American poet John Crowe Ransom. The MacMillan edition of the *Collected Poems of Thomas Hardy* had just been published and we had to have that for the course. I remember at one lecture, Ransom talked vaguely about form and meter and stood up at the front of the class going "pom, pom, pom" through the poem. He then said that for the next class he wanted everyone to choose poems from the collection that would fill about eight pages in an anthology and to come prepared to defend the choices. He then questioned our selections and why no two lists were the same. It was a great discussion because you had to defend your list against everyone else's. At the end of the seminar he announced that he was about to honour an agreement to choose eight pages of Hardy poetry for an anthology of British verse and said, "thank you all very much." (Laughter).

Interviewers: Why did you not publish a collection of your own work until Winter Sun *in 1960?*

Avison: *Winter Sun* was rejected twelve times before it was accepted. That was the reason.

I published a lot in little magazines. But what I didn't want to do in the days of *First Statement* and the *Northern Review* was to publish prematurely. In those days anything that anyone wanted made its way into print. I didn't like that.

Interviewers: But you did manage to attract a critical reputation before you had a collection published. Milton Wilson wrote about your work in the first issue of Canadian Literature *in 1958.*

Avison: I didn't realize it appeared as early as that.

Interviewers: He called you a poet of "negative legend."

Avison: That's about what it amounts to — a negative legend. It was the sort of thing — "Here you are, can you prove it?"

Interviewers: Cid Corman, the American poet and editor living in Japan, featured some of your work in his magazine Origin. *How did that come about?*

Avison: Through the readings that Raymond Souster organized here in Toronto, Souster introduced us. The readings were at the Isaacs Gallery and at the YMHA (Young Men's Hebrew Association) at Bloor and Spadina. I lived about a block away on Washington Avenue. I had a reception after one of the readings there and that's when I got to know all those people such as Denise Levertov. While he was in Toronto, Corman came to some of the readings and collected work from people he liked. There was a fascination going on then for the long poem and I had the Agnes Cleves piece.

Interviewers: Who was Agnes Cleves?

Avison: Agnes Cleves never existed. It is too bad to invent a woman like that. The truth of the matter is that that was "beer poetry." I stopped writing it because there was a weekend when I didn't have any beer and I couldn't write. I was working, and I'd come home tired and disenchanted, and have a few beers, and I'd start writing anything I wanted. And that's how Agnes Cleves came about. The people in it are a lot of the people I was working with then.

Interviewers: Where were you working?

Avison: I won't tell. (Laughter).

Interviewers: You mention Denise Levertov. Frank Davey says he sees affinities between your work and hers.

Avison: Levertov and I both got preachy — she in the cause of peace and me in promoting the Christian faith. But you know, I always felt from the beginning that the biggest influence on me was the American poet, Elizabeth Bishop. I realized after I had read her work that I had memorised most of it by heart. It all sounded so familiar to me, even her prose about the Depression era — it could have been about me. You know, it's all about living in the city, struggling against poverty, trying to preserve a little time for writing.

Interviewers: That seems to be what the poems in Winter Sun *are about.*

Avison: Yes, that's what they say. I graduated from university with a gold medal and no cash: that's been the story of my life. I started out as a paper jogger in a factory, and I've been earning my living ever since from such jobs. I got the Governor General's Award for Poetry in 1960, but that was the last year before it had any money attached to it. It has been like that all the way through, but I never applied for a Canada Council grant because I think it is a misuse of their money. I've been campaigning with the Council from the start to set up a

Canadian distribution system for books and magazines — to get Canadian books into airports and bus stations and small stores, and to have kiosks with literature. They should be spending all the Canada Council money on that and not on individual writers. Let the writers earn their living from what they write. But this can only happen when their works are given wide popular distribution. There isn't any circulation now, really, except to people who have the schooling to learn that it is there. The people who want to read never discover it. I knew one woman poet who never had any poetic model except the Coutts greeting cards. Her life was a sad story because that's all she really got to know. You have to have wider distribution. Even in the cities, people don't go to the high-tone places, they go to their neighbourhood stores. I've never lived off my poetry. I've supported myself with a nine-to-five job. This allows me to take part in the real world. Poetry doesn't put bread on the table, and anyway, I'm a workaholic.

Interviewers: You published a lot of your early work in the United States. Was that because there were so few Canadian markets at the time?

Avison: Partly. But also, partly, because I didn't like the business in Canada of everyone publishing everything just because it existed and was Canadian.

Interviewers: Between Winter Sun *and* The Dumbfounding, *there is a marked change in your approach, your style, and your content in your poetry. This has been attributed to certain things that happened to you in 1963. Could you talk about that shift?*

Avison: I was an agnostic in *Winter Sun* and a believer in *The Dumbfounding*.

Interviewers: A.J.M. Smith calls what took place "a precisely dated mystical experience."

Avison: January 4, 1963. For two years I had been drifting in and out of churches because everything was getting greyer. It all started because of a crazy encounter I had while I was working with Kathleen Coburn on the Coleridge papers at the University of Toronto. She sent me down to the women's washroom in Emmanuel College to correct the proofs for her book while she interviewed someone from a publishing house. I was sitting there, smoking, and correcting these proofs when this woman walked in and said, "Do you know the joy of knowing the Lord Jesus?" I looked up with the pen in one hand and a cigarette in the other and said: "I know the theory, but as you can see, I'm busy." I still remember thinking, "I'm nicer than that." When she didn't go away I looked up to apologise and her face was just shining with a radiance, and she said, "I have never been beset by doubt." This was a kind of lingo I hadn't heard. She invited me to her church, and I said no thank you but she told me where it was and eventually I decided to go. I went to the church and I began to read Ezekiel while I was sitting there. Nobody spoke to me and I was very grateful.

Interviewers: What was the church?

Avison: Knox Presbyterian on Spadina Avenue. Finally, I leaned across to a woman and I said: "You people talk about faith but you've got it and I don't. What am I supposed to do?" She replied "Go talk to the minister." He, mostly, got me upset but said one thing I really remember: "If faith was something that you could work out with your head, it wouldn't be worth going after." That stayed in my mind. He made me promise to read through the Gospel of John. So I did. There was one morning I read doggedly on and I got to 14:1, "If you believe in God, you believe also in me." It was as if I heard a voice out of the words and I couldn't go any further. I thought, "Yes, I believe in God, so the rest must follow." But I made it conditional and said it out loud:

"You can have everything but leave me the poetry. It is all I've got." Then suddenly it was like being inside an eggshell. Everything was motionless, colourless, a world of nothing. I threw my Bible and it crashed against the window. I said: "Okay, take the poetry too!" That was it. And I looked at my desk, and it was as if there were iron filings just smashed all over the top. When I threw the Bible, I guess that was the crack in the eggshell. Gradually, the iron filings on the desk began to arrange themselves into geometrical shapes and patterns, and when I saw that I called the minister and said, "I now believe!" And he said, "That's nice. I'll see you Sunday." (Laughter). I was very disappointed.

Interviewers: What, exactly, were the filings doing?

Avison: They were a mess of brokenness in the beginning and then order afterwards. I knew there was really nothing on the desk. But I saw them! And I started believing from that moment, helplessly. It was *the* moment in my life. I tried to block it with all my power. I remember during the period approaching that day thinking that the one thing I did not want was everlasting life. I wanted it to end soon. It was the one thing I had not bargained for.

Interviewers: It seems that after the conversion the whole style of your poetry changed — the line lengths became shorter, the diction became clearer, the images more vivid. There doesn't seem to be the same linguistic struggling going on in The Dumbfounding *as one sees in* Winter Sun.

Avison: Yes, but I don't know how much of that is conviction and how much is simply poetic maturity. I think there is a certain kind of lyrical poetry that is particular to the very young. If they go on writing, they usually abandon it. My feeling when I was writing in my teens and twenties was that my very limited human experience was my whole world, and in the moments of self-awareness I could write poetry. The maturity came about at that moment of knowing what I didn't know, and the excitement of knowing what I didn't know was greater back then.

Interviewers: Several of the poems in Sunblue *appear to be commentaries on Biblical passages with an epigraph or title containing or giving reference numbers to certain verses.*

Avison: Yes, that is an old Medieval device known as a "meditation." It hasn't been done much since so it seems like something new. I'm not improving on anything; I'm just absorbing it. The theory behind it is that the Bible is its own commentary, and that the context for any given quotation is the whole Bible.

Interviewers: You've recently become involved in the censorship issue regarding the banning by the Peterborough School Board of Margaret Laurence's books. How do you, as a fundamentalist, view other fundamentalists wanting to ban literature?

Avison: I am against book-banning. I am also against pornography as Margaret Laurence is. That is why I support her. What it comes down to is that the purity of God is inaccessible. The cross is God becoming accessible — becoming involved in us through His death. He is made available to us by this, and, therefore, you have to take up your cross in order to become involved with Him. It is the opposite of what the book-banning crowd is doing. They don't want to become involved. Literature demands involvement.

Interviewers: Therefore, you are saying, that the book-banning crowd is denying the sanctity of the word…

Avison: I didn't say that. You have to keep the faith from degenerating into a sub-culture. I'm not a relativist. The Gospel is intolerant. There is one way. The book-banning people are a minority. The faith should not be a clique or a sub-culture. It should not be a minority opinion because it is a Truth.

Interviewers: But at the same time it has to be an active truth moving within the world.

Avison: Right. You can't use it as an opinion to club people with.

Interviewers: There are many ethical and moral issues confronting Christians today, such as the whole area of biomedical ethics…

Avison: Yes, like what has happened to my mother. She is one-hundred and two and is in Riverdale Hospital.* I believe her life is being prolonged unnecessarily — falsely, and against God's will. She has congestive heart failure and suffered a cardiac arrest. I asked the doctors not to revive her. They did. She isn't aware of who she is or where she is because the circulation to her brain was disrupted. She is very uncomfortable and she is a nuisance to medical support systems. This is the fruit of technology and I'm against it. Her death has been robbed of its dignity. And I see other cases all around her in the hospital.

Interviewers: In your poetry you've always said that Christianity has to be an active force in coming to terms with one's problems.

Avison: And the problem in my mother's case is coming to terms with death. They kept asking me at the hospital, "What's your philosophy?" And I'd say "Hezekiah's poultice." They had never heard of that. Hezekiah's poultice refers to the story of an Old Testament king of Israel who fell ill and wanted Isaiah to come and visit him and tell him whether or not he was going to die. And the Lord said to Isaiah "Tell him it is a sickness unto death." So Hezekiah turned his face to the wall and whimpered, "No Lord, I've been a good king, please let me live," and the Lord said to Isaiah, "Apply this poultice and he'll get better." And Hezekiah did. Then for the next fifteen years of his life he betrayed Israel to the Assyrians. Great story. So the sovereignty of God in that was, "Yes you will die," but he couldn't accomplish that. It is our choice, you know, to accept or to fight it off and if you believe then something tells you when to do which.

[* *Margaret Avison's mother died the following June.*]

The Possibility of Possibilities:

Neil Bissoondath

After struggling through a heavy midwinter Montreal snowfall, and up a steep flight of ice-covered steps to what appeared to be almost a second-floor entrance way, we rang the doorbell and waited for an answer. Neil Bissoondath opened the door. He was dressed in a white sweater, white shirt, and blue jeans. He was holding the nozzle of a vacuum cleaner. "I've just been frantically tidying up before you arrived," he apologised. He showed us into the living room furnished with low futon couches, crowded wicker bookshelves, and hanging oriental rugs over snow white walls. The place was impeccably clean.

Bissoondath disappeared down a long corridor into his kitchen and emerged with a bottle of red wine, three glasses, and a package of string cheese. "I know it looks strange, but it is quite good. My wife, who is a French Canadian, tells me that this is a local favourite as a snack in the bars around here. I'm still getting used to some of the more subtle things about Montreal," he told us as he lay back on the low couch, and let out the first of many infectious laughs as we struggled to untwine the ball of cheese.

In his works, Neil Bissoondath is fascinated by characters who are in transition — individuals in the process of adjusting to their environments, or struggling to escape them; yet Bissoondath exudes an aura of self-assured, relaxed confidence, in both his manner and speech. Neil Bissoondath was born in Trinidad in 1955 and came to Canada as a student in 1973 to study French at York University. Before becoming a full-time writer, he taught English and French as a second language at a private school in Toronto. His works include two collections of short stories, *Digging Up The Mountains* (1985), *On the Eve of Uncertain Tomorrows* (1991), and the novel *A Casual Brutality* (1988). This interview was conducted on February 6, 1989, in Montreal.

Interviewers: In Andrew Gerrod's Speaking for Myself, *you said that* A Casual Brutality *might be your last book with a Trinidadian setting and that you were interested in moving on to writing about Spain, for instance. Do you still feel that way?*

Bissoondath: Oh yes, absolutely. I don't anticipate writing another novel about the West Indies. I have written some short stories recently, and some are set in the West Indies and deal with West Indians. I'm planning a trip to Spain for this year to do preliminary research for a non-fiction book that I have in mind — the sort of book that could combine fiction and non-fiction.

Interviewers: A travel book?

Bissoondath: It won't be easy to fit the book into a particular genre. It will be partly a travel book, partly a history book, partly fiction and partly non-fiction.

Interviewers: Why the interest in Spain?

Bissoondath: It is something I don't understand. It is part of the reason I look forward to going back to Spain to solve the mystery. I went to Spain in the first place because I have two good friends from Barcelona. The son was studying English in Toronto at the school where I was teaching, and so we became friends. His father came during the summer, and since I was one of the people around who was able to speak Spanish I accompanied them on various trips around the province. They invited me to visit them in Spain, which I did after the first cheque from *Digging Up the Mountains*. I flew into Madrid and a funny thing happened when I got off the plane and was standing in the immigration line at the terminal. There were *Guardia Civil* armed with submachine guns standing out on the tarmac. Standing in that line, however, I felt incredibly at home. I

usually hate such line-ups but this was different. (Laughter). As I travelled around the country to Toledo, and Barcelona, and Madrid, I continued to feel at home. Wherever I go in Spain, for some curious reason, I feel I belong there.

Interviewers: What is it that fascinates you about Spain?

Bissoondath: Well, intellectually, I'm fascinated by the history, by the politics, especially the formation of Spain by the reconquest from the Moors by Isabella and Ferdinand. The problems we see in Spain today can be directly traced back to the unification agreements that were made in the fifteenth century; the regionalism, the Catalan question, all have their roots in that period. But there's also an emotional component to my fascination that I don't understand. Of course, people have mentioned things such as reincarnation. I don't believe in that, thank you very much. I'm not prepared to accept something on faith. I'm not prepared to say I believe in something unless I have solid physical proof.

Interviewers: Are you interested in Spanish writing?

Bissoondath: Not particularly. Spanish writing in this century, since the civil war, has not been very exciting. The Spanish language writing that has interested me has been done in South America. Spain, I have found out, is now beginning to produce new and exciting writing, but that has taken the death of Franco, and the cultural explosion that has taken place there recently. At the same time, my favourite poet is Federico Garcia Lorca. He has always spoken to me in a very emotional way that no other poet has.

Interviewers: Why?

Bissoondath: I don't know. This is part of the mystery.

Interviewers: But his language is so direct, and his images so sharp.

Bissoondath: And his language is at the same time so musical. I lose myself in listening to the sound of the words themselves, and just dream.

Interviewers: You mentioned how some of the tensions in Spain have their origins deep in history, especially in the amalgamation of so many various groups, languages, and even races. One of the important features of your work is the uncovering and the description of racial tensions. You have, however, made it quite clear that you disagree strongly with the multicultural government policies in Canada, feeling that these policies are driving people apart rather than bringing them together. If you have your way, what would you like to see in place of these policies?

Bissoondath: What I would like would be to have no official policy. I believe in a certain amount of government intervention to point people in certain directions, but that's just to nudge people rather than to demand that people maintain their former cultures. People arrive in this country and their attitude is almost one of belligerence. They say, "well, I am here, I am Jamaican, Trinidadian, whatever, and the government has this policy, and I have the absolute right to behave my way and act a certain way." West Indians will have incredibly disruptive parties, and when there are complaints, then their attitude is, "What the hell, I have the right."

Interviewers: Like in your story "Dancing" in Digging Up the Mountains.

Bissoondath: Right. There is this unwillingness to compromise. This springs from their belief that they don't have to live here as Canadians. They believe that they are here to carry on their culture. And this is a false thing in the end. After ten years in this country, you are no longer a Trinidadian or a Jamaican, you have changed in ways you can't always appreciate. If you keep telling yourself that you have to behave in certain ways, then you end up making a stereotype of yourself.

Interviewers: Then there's the problem with people who have been here three, four, or five generations. They suddenly feel that they are culturally displaced. But you don't subscribe to the American melting pot theory either, do you?

Bissoondath: No, I don't subscribe to that. I don't think you can shrug off what you have been. You can't throw off your parent's culture after growing up in their house. There's got to be a middle road. I knew a girl who grew up in Toronto but kept describing herself as Russian. Then she made a trip to the Soviet Union, and could hardly wait to get back. She spoke the language, as her parents had done, but she was not Russian. Culturally, she was informed. But personally, she was not what she had thought she was. She was Canadian. This is the problem with people who grow up here and are told that they are something other than Canadian. They grow up with festivals such as Caravan in Toronto, and they dress up in costumes and pretend to be something they are not. And for people not of these cultures who go and watch them dancing around on the stage and eating over-priced food — what do they get from this? What do they learn about these cultures? Nothing. They just see the stereotype.

Interviewers: So, you obviously don't see yourself as a Trinidadian-Canadian.

Bissoondath: I reject all these terms such as "immigrant," "New Canadian," a "hyphenated-Canadian." They all imply that you don't belong yet, that you are not Canadian. The

Americans, by contrast, have ingested the whole immigrant experience. They mythologised all of that. It is fully part of their history. In Canada, we want to hide it, in a way, because it is not a fully-integrated part of our history. It sets anyone who has been involved in immigration apart. I don't like this sense of "apartness." I want to belong. I feel I belong. Regardless of where I've been in this country, English or French Canada, East or West, I've felt at home.

Interviewers: Do you draw a distinction between multiculturalism policies and the handling of race relations?

Bissoondath: Yes I do. I actually feel fairly relaxed about race relations. From my understanding of how Canada has worked as a country, there have always been periods of tension when new groups arrived. And the tensions inevitably give way. That will happen with those who are arriving now. I see no reason for that not to happen. Where it becomes dangerous is when the group that becomes the victim of a certain amount of racism starts seeing racism where it is not. It is an easy thing to scream racism every time something happens, and that inevitably sets back the process of acceptance. That gets peoples' backs up.

Interviewers: Isn't there a certain security in portraying oneself as a victim?

Bissoondath: Of course. This is part of the problem you're seeing in Toronto these days. There are some people who for personal or professional or psychological reasons need to feel themselves victims. It is not only non-whites. There are also whites who feel the need to see themselves as racists. It stuns me when I run into someone who is white who says "this is an incredibly racist society." What are you telling me?, I say to them. That this is a racist society and everyone who lives here is a racist? It is simply not so.

Interviewers: You pointed out in an article in the Toronto Star *that racism is as "Canadian as maple syrup, as American as apple pie…"*

Bissoondath: And in Jamaica as Jamaican as...

Interviewers: That seems to come out in your stories about Trinidad, where there is a tension between the Blacks and the Asians, the Blacks and the Whites, the Whites and the Asians.

Bissoondath: Yes, racism exists everywhere. I think Trinidad is a far more racist society than here in Canada. The character of Surein in *A Casual Brutality* is based on many people I knew in Trinidad. They'd walk around with knives in their boots, and they had axe handles in their cars. And they will tell you that this stuff is to protect themselves against the "niggers." And that's the phrase East Indians use for Blacks down there.

Interviewers: What makes it less violent and virulent here?

Bissoondath: Part of the strength, and at the same time the weakness, of Canadian society, is the urge to compromise, the urge to diffuse situations. When there are racial problems there is a lot of good will out there. People get together and think: what are we going to do to remedy this situation? There's a certain urge to goodwill, and that has helped a great deal.

Interviewers: Or a sense of indifference that we never do anything by halves that can be done by quarters?

Bissoondath: No, I don't think it's indifference. I think, at times, there is too much of a readiness to compromise. As I am saying this, I am always impressed in Toronto by the way the police and the government react to deal with the causes of the problems.

I'm not saying they have the answers or that they are doing a particularly good job, but the urge is there. I would describe myself as a proud Canadian. Wherever I go, I make sure that people know I am not anything other than a Canadian. I will not accept any other label.

Interviewers: As you were talking, we were reminded of the conclusion of A Casual Brutality where Raj is clearly trying to make a clean break with the colonial past of his country. He says, "I go like my forebears to the future, to the challenge that lies elsewhere, of turning nothing into something, far from the casual brutality of collapse, far from the ruins of failure..." There is a suggestion at the conclusion, that the syndrome of the Third World 'tin pot' dictator, is a direct result of colonialism — that the worst aspects of colonialism are being imitated by such individuals.

Bissoondath: It is the only way I can understand why the Third World has gone the way it has.

Interviewers: There were no other moral examples?

Bissoondath: The idea everyone was left with was that the country was there to be raped. A country existed so that those who could, would enrich themselves. This was the basic drive behind colonialism. I think there were other ideas that the British tried to transmit, and you can see these in things such as the fact that India is more or less a democratic society today. Most of the former British colonies became independent as functioning parliamentary democracies. But those elements were easily thrown off because the urge to greed was much more attractive. While acknowledging that fact, I won't excuse Third World dictatorships and elites for what they have done because many of these countries have been independent for twenty-five years now, a whole generation. Many in that generation have gone abroad, they've got the education, they know about western democracy, but they have not established democracies at home. The urge to enrich themselves, as in the colonial past, is too strong. So, I think the matter is not as simple as blaming the British or the Americans or the French or whoever for all the problems today in the Third World. Things are a lot more complex. They (the Third World) must accept some of the blame, too. Blaming the colonial past is just an easy way of trying to excuse the Third World from its own responsibility.

Interviewers: There's the sense in some of the stories in Digging Up the Mountains that tourists come to the Third World to take something from the places they visit.

Bissoondath: Yes, that's right. A lot of these countries, lack pride in themselves. I think if they had a sense of themselves, they would not rape themselves. People there would understand that there is much to be done beyond enriching themselves. You need the idea of building something, and in order to achieve anything there has to be a certain amount of self-sacrifice. So, when you don't have that pride, when the tourist arrives, people begin to see themselves as just slaves once again. They don't see the tourist as someone bringing badly needed money into the place.

Interviewers: Is there also the sense that the people on the islands feel trapped there, whereas the tourist can come and go?

Bissoondath: I don't know how general an attitude that is. Some would like to go, certainly. But I don't think that's the central problem.

Interviewers: There is that strong sense of entrapment though, in the story "The Cage" where the Japanese language student in Toronto is still very burdened by her cultural upbringing. You once said in an interview that "The Cage" reminded you of your own upbringing. Could you elaborate on that?

Bissoondath: Yes. I grew up in a culture that restricted me, a culture that imposed its values on me, and that had little regard for my personal feelings and desires. From that point of view, I identify with that Japanese girl very closely. I grew up in Trinidad where the family itself was wide open. The Naipaul family always read a lot. I remember my mother always reading two or three books, and I got my love of reading from her. We travelled a great deal, so I was aware of the wider world. But at the same time, living in that family, and on the small island of Trinidad, you couldn't get all the things that we knew existed. Our relatives travelled, we knew everything that was out there, but we had no access to them. I was aware from an early age that our main sources of news were *Time* magazine and the BBC — there's a lot more than that out there. I remember being impatient with that at a young age. So I grew up with that sense of being held back. Also, on a personal level, I could never accept those values being imposed on me. Reading, of course, is a solitary act, and you need quiet and time for that. But in the extended family, that quiet and that personal time was never respected. People dropped by and simply expected to be entertained. If you refused to be a host, well, it was a small place and word got around fast. You ended up with a bad reputation.

Interviewers: And that situation is described in A Casual Brutality.

Bissoondath: Right. And it is something I identify with. I hated that sort of thing but it was something I had to do. I had to kiss the relatives I didn't know and didn't like. I had to pretend all the time. That impatience with

that kind of a position is something I can identify with very much, like the girl in "The Cage" who can't escape her past. It is a question I've been thinking about a great deal lately — how much can you escape the cultural imperative? I've had to be, myself, rather harsh to preserve my independence. When I left Trinidad, I knew I was leaving for good. I only went back reluctantly to visit my parents a couple of times after I left. Now that my family is no longer there I have no desire to return to Trinidad. None. I think my parents probably had a tough time trying to understand why I didn't want to go back to the island to visit them every summer. My mother, I think, accepted it more easily than my father did. I knew I was causing pain, but I was aware that I had to live my own life. That girl in "The Cage," in the end, was incapable of saying that. I don't quite know why, because I don't understand everything about her. I don't think I understand everything about any of my characters. But she was from the Japanese culture and I think that is why she returned: there's a particularly powerful link. I experienced, myself, that kind of sense of alienation as an immigrant when I first came here. I remember walking into the university cafeteria, and seeing the South Asians in one corner, the Whites in another, the Chinese in a third, and the West Indians in another. I suddenly realised I was expected to eat lunch with "my own kind." This was my first experience of what I came to see as multiculturalism in Canada — people set apart rather than coming together. The West Indians sat around and talked about reggae music and plans for their next party. I wasn't interested in either of these things. I wanted to approach people as individuals.

Interviewers: It sounds like the story, "The Revolutionary," in Digging Up the Mountains.

Bissoondath: Yes, that's right. There are some biographical elements in that story.

Interviewers: What is your expectation of your readers' understanding of your characters?

Bissoondath: I would hope they would understand them as well as I do, but in fact, often I find they have a better understanding. That's why I enjoy doing readings and answering questions and hearing comments, because I actually learn a lot myself about my characters. That's the joy of it. I wouldn't want to tell the reader everything. I wouldn't want to pretend to.

Interviewers: Of course, they're just rebuilding them according to your instructions.

Bissoondath: Yes. But they bring to them all kinds of extra things I couldn't. My readers interpret things according to their own experiences.

Interviewers: A lot of readers and reviewers have interpreted the conclusion of A Casual Brutality as being quite pessimistic. How do you respond to that?

Bissoondath: I'm an optimist and I think that ending was optimistic. The very fact that Raj has another chance, that his life continues, and that he realises that he has the chance to "make something out of nothing," is to me, optimistic — but realistically optimistic. I don't see myself capable of having trumpets blaring at the end of a story because I don't think life works that way. Realism is more important to me than anything else.

Interviewers: Is that the sense of "so it has been, so it shall be?"

Bissoondath: Yes. It is the character realising the possibility of possibility. So, it is not an easy optimism. I don't think anyone could be a writer if he were a pessimist because, simply, why write if you are a pessimist? Why start in the first place.

Interviewers: To warn, as Wilfred Owen said?

Bissoondath: Yes, but why bother warning?

Interviewers: In relation to the sense of warning, it seems that throughout A Casual Brutality, Raj is being warned about Madera, but he seems to ignore the warnings; he is very passive.

Bissoondath: Well, this is because he knew him back in school and he didn't take him seriously then, and he finds it hard ever to take him seriously. The same Madera who just shook his biceps at school is the same one who Raj continues to see.

Interviewers: He's a bully…

Bissoondath: Yes, but now a bully with a gun. You know the section of the novel which deals with Madera at school was originally a short story that I had thought of including in *Digging Up The Mountains*. So, that is really a set-piece. It fell so naturally into the novel that I decided to leave it in.

Interviewers: For you, how does the process of writing a short story differ from that of writing a novel?

Bissoondath: The thing with short stories is that they simply come to me. I will get a feeling more than anything else: there's a story inside waiting to be told. It could be a line of dialogue, or it could be a strange image I have. I just know it's there. I'll just sit down and start writing. It could turn out to be a twenty page short story or it could turn out to be a novel. I just finished a short story that's thirty-nine pages long. No one's going to take that. Magazines want stories that are a certain length, no more than and no less than. I can't write that way. My short stories turn out to be fairly long, and A Casual Brutality just turned out to be one hell of a long short story.

Interviewers: How did A Casual Brutality *begin for you?*

Bissoondath: The first scene I visualised was Raj seeing his grandmother. When I started writing I wasn't sure what the voice was going to be. It took me a while. I started writing it in the third person singular past. It just wouldn't work. It only began to work when I tried Raj speaking. What I kept hearing was Raj's voice but I couldn't identify it. Form imposes itself too, you know.

Interviewers: How do you mean? You have a lot of flashbacks, for instance, in the novel.

Bissoondath: I didn't decide on that. It imposed itself.

Interviewers: You've said that there was one story of yours where you actually cut up and moved the pieces around: "An Arrangement of Shadows."

Bissoondath: Yes, because it was fairly unruly in the way it came out. So I had to sit down once the text was done and cut and paste. But the last story in *Digging Up the Mountains*, "Counting the Wind," has a strange form, first person to third person, present to past. It just keeps moving from section to section. When I first started writing that story it moved very quickly. I wrote the first section and it was in one person and one tense. And then, for no reason, the story switched to another person and another tense. So I let the story dictate itself according to its own pace. I thought, well, in the end I'll go back and change it all once I had it finished. Instead, I gave it to my editor and she loved it. It is just the way the story shaped itself. I wasn't really experimenting with various devices. That's the way I like to work.

Interviewers: How do you know, though, which passages to move around?

Bissoondath: It is a question of dissatisfaction. I just know when certain things aren't going to work, and there has to be cutting and taping. When the story is well-balanced, there is a sense of satisfaction. You know the thing fits.

Interviewers: There are a lot of flashbacks that appear in your work. The traditional wisdom is that readers lose interest if there are a lot of flashbacks in that they naturally want to see the story move along.

Bissoondath: Well, I think flashbacks do move the story along.

Interviewers: As in Laurence Sterne's little diagrams of narrative progression in Tristram Shandy — *some are all twisted like this strange knotted string cheese we're eating. (Laughter).*

Bissoondath: I never thought of that! (Laughter). Literary cheese! There we go...But this is part of my impatience with television. My experience in trying to adapt one of my stories for television is that television people don't believe in flashbacks or dreams. I find it strange that television writers believe that people can't deal with dreams. There's an amazing urge to underestimate the viewer. Perhaps there is a fear of dreams on television because they inhabit the realm beyond our control. Fiction, too, is beyond our control; but at least we have the illusion that we are in control. But with dreams we have no control. Dreams will do with you what they wish.

Interviewers: Flashbacks in your story often involve remembrances of family incidents and histories...

Bissoondath: Well, you know, I probably do that because I'm very ambivalent about family as a concept. While I am very close to my immediate family, I am more suspicious of the extended family, of the tribe, which, in my experience, tries to impose its visions, its values, its ways of doing things. But this transcends the family. It goes to the idea of the group in general. I don't like joining groups. I don't like belonging to organisations. I can't bring myself to have a membership card in anything, including family. Maybe it's an attempt to escape a certain responsibility. If you agree to belong to a group, you immediately have certain responsibilities to fulfil. Growing up in Trinidad, I was the only member of a platoon of cousins who enjoyed reading. I remember going to the beach in the summer with the cousins and they would go off hunting, fishing, but I was loathe to put my book down. And that created problems for them in leaving me behind. My solitary reading was insulting to them. They thought that by not joining them I was saying that their activity wasn't good enough for me — or at least that was their attitude. But my attitude was simply that I was an individual first and not a member of a group. That's very important to me. If people's expectations of you make them uncomfortable with you, then that's too bad for them.

Interviewers: There's that sense of the paramount importance of the individual in the character of Raj in A Casual Brutality. *But, to what degree is there a sense of self-realisation, self-recognition?*

Bissoondath: I'd like to think that at the end Raj has learned a lesson. That's why, again, I think there's optimism in that ending.

Interviewers: But maybe what he's coming to is a sense that he doesn't want to be responsible for anyone other than himself.

Bissoondath: I think he may. I don't know.

Interviewers: The story "Continental Drift," in Digging Up The Mountains, *is about a student traveller in Europe who doesn't want to have any*

responsibilities and connections. How did that story come about?

Bissoondath: That comes from a night I spent in a youth hostel in Bordeaux. It was just my observations of people who were floating around. And it deals with that same sensation I had. I never back-packed. I was in Bordeaux to go to the university. Something screwed up my arrangements so I had to spend a night in a youth hostel while the university got the details straight. There were some strange characters, but they weren't quite as dangerous as I depicted them. It was just the idea of strangers meeting each other, what people are looking for. People who have been travelling for months will sit and tell you they no longer remember what they've seen where. Their hearts weren't in it anymore but they couldn't help doing it either. They'd say they'd eventually return home, but they weren't sure when. There were different Europeans travelling around looking for jobs. The story came out of that strange night.

Interviewers: Another story that interested us in regard to its genesis was "An Arrangement of Shadows."

Bissoondath: That is not based on any biographical elements. It is just pure imagination. It started with the image of the clock-tower where the hands had stopped, and I simply described what I saw. As the story went along, I discovered more and more about Miss Jackson, the central character. She just came into the story. It was a very unconscious story. Another story that was like that was "There Are A Lot of Ways to Die." It is not based on any kind of reality that I can identify with. That one began with the image of the sign, 'Joseph Heaven: Carpet and Rug Installations.' The sign in the story is connected with the image of the dilapidated colonial mansion, the Pacheco House. I suppose some of the story comes from my knowledge of people who have gone back to the islands from places like Toronto, who think, 'well, now I'm in a position to go tell these poor fools what they really should be doing with their lives, and make things good and be their saviour.' But that's not what it is all about in the island. You think you are going to be welcomed with open arms but really you are seeking a certain status. By breaking the window in the Pacheco House at the conclusion of the story, Joseph Heaven sets himself free, which gets back to what I was saying earlier about immigrants: you have to let go of the past. You cannot allow that to hold you back as it does in "The Cage." This is vital. You can be caught by both a wider historical cultural past and a familial past.

Interviewers: You say, at the beginning of A Casual Brutality, *that "the word hope is at times but a synonym for illusion: it is the most virile of perils." Is this the condition of Raj?*

Bissoondath: I don't think so. I think this is how we should view the nation of Casaquemada, the fictional setting for the novel. I don't think that phrase is tied to any individual character. It applies to a certain extent to Grappler — he just continues on regardless. The Grappler kind of man is now leaving the islands. It is the whole idea of what I was saying earlier about reality, about reality being very important to me. I'm a realistic optimist as opposed to a blind optimist. Blind optimists say no matter what happens, I'll be fine. That's dangerous. That's dangerous because it blinds you to what is actually happening to you. It blinds you to the consequences of your actions. You have to distinguish between the two. Illusion is the most dangerous thing. Hope is a necessary part of human life but illusion is incredibly, incredibly dangerous.

Interviewers: Yet someone like Miss Jackson in "An Arrangement of Shadows" is living in a state of illusion.

Bissoondath: She is.

Interviewers: She's like something from Paul Scott's Raj Quartet — Bobby, *who seems to think she can civilise India according to the British colonial ideal.*

Bissoondath: The illusion of colonialism was that it was supposed to be casting the shadow of democracy and civilisation. The reality was what was really transmitted in the end.

Nothing Better Than Poetry?:

We had just returned from an unusually warm weekend in Saskatchewan in December 1988 during which Lorna Crozier had launched her new collection, *Angels of Flesh, Angels of Silence* at a brunch in a downtown Saskatoon restaurant. In the busy hours of a weekend that included our interview with Patrick Lane, we had not found the time to photograph Crozier and we agreed to meet her on the following Tuesday at a book shop where she was signing copies of her collection. We walked down the street with her in search of a good background and came across a brightly coloured fruit and vegetable store that spread its wares out onto Yonge Street's sidewalk.

Interviewers: Here's a good spot, right in front of the fruit and vegetables. "The Sex Lives of Vegetables?" A bit too cute?

Crozier: Gee, well, whatever you want. (Laughter). I'm open to suggestions. (She stands with her back to the sidewalk display). I'm always a bit nervous about photographs.

Interviewers: Just think of all the fun those veggies are having behind you. You should see what they're doing. Sweet potatoes. Carrots. Turnips. (Crozier breaks into a wide grin. Suddenly an old woman who just happens to be walking along the street trailing a bundle-buggy of groceries and vegetables behind her slugs Meyer with her purse. Meyer does not look up from the lens of his camera and continues to shoot. The old woman walks on).

Crozier: That woman...she just hit you! Do you know her? Have you ever seen her before?

Interviewers: No.

Crozier: Does this sort of thing happen all the time in Toronto?

Interviewers: Yes.

Lorna Crozier

Lorna Crozier, whose *Angels of Flesh, Angels of Silence* was nominated for the 1988 Governor General's Award for Poetry, was born in Swift Current, Saskatchewan in 1948, and following a career as a high school teacher, a guidance counsellor, a writer-in-residence, and a government worker, she teaches at the University of Saskatchewan in Saskatoon. Her works include *Inside the Sky* (1976), *Crow's Black Joy* (1978), *Humans and Other Beasts* (1980), *No Longer Two People* (1981, which she co-wrote with Patrick Lane, with whom she lives), *The Weather* (1984), *The Garden Going On Without Us* (1987), and *Angels of Flesh, Angels of Silence* (1988). This interview was conducted while Crozier was visiting Toronto in March 1988 and additional information was added during our trip to Saskatchewan in December 1988.

Interviewers: There's a sort of metaphysical mathematics to your poems, a sense of all the images adding up but not to what you'd expect. Are you striving for this in your poems, such as in "Forms of Innocence" or "The Horizon is a Line"?

Crozier: The question is what is deliberate and what isn't. Nothing seems deliberate when I begin a poem because I have no idea at all where it is going or where it is going to end up, or even what I want to write about until it is already written. It's only in the revision process that I try to hone the images and take advantage of what is recurring and overlapping. I'm glad you said they add up to something you don't expect because otherwise they'd be quite boring, to me as well as you.

Interviewers: So you are just as surprised to what they add up to as the reader?

Crozier: I find it interesting to see where I've ended up. Favourite poems of mine are ones in which I give a bizarre or unexpected slant to things. I don't think in terms of metaphysical conceits, but the poems that work best for me are the ones where cabbages become turtles, and when the ordinary object becomes magical or different or unusual.

Interviewers: A metamorphosis?

Crozier: Yeah. And yet I hope I am being true to the object itself, like a carrot isn't a turtle but a cabbage is — a correspondence of shape and pattern — and it is as much a turtle as it is a cabbage. I want to *see* clearly rather than impose my view. I want to be true to the qualities, the characteristics of things, and the essences of things in that metamorphosis. The poems that please me the most are the ones where I've looked at something and seen it in a way I don't think it has been seen before.

Interviewers: It's not so much making direct connections with something else, it's a leap in imagination.

Crozier: That's what excites me. It's what excited me about Neruda's "Ode to Socks", which is one of my favourite poems. The conceit in that poem is taken all the way from a simple pair of wool socks, to firemen, to all these wonderful bizarre comparisons that he *discovered*; a matter of seeing what's there rather than simply putting something there.

Interviewers: In your poem, "The Photograph I Keep of Them," one is reminded of Atwood's "This is a Photograph of Me." Is that a deliberate connection you want us to make?

Crozier: The photo that I describe is one that I actually have on my desk. I suppose the mythology present is that of the Depression, the 'Dirty Thirties.' Although I wasn't born then, I grew up with those stories about that time. Every time I'd complain about something, I'd be told, "You should have grown up during the Depression — we only had flour sacks for pyjamas, and we got one Jap orange (we didn't call them Mandarin) for Christmas." In every photograph my parents have of the Thirties, my relatives are always posing in front of cars. The metaphoric possibilities of that are splendid. In the past, at least, people born on the Prairies have wanted to get out. People like Mandel, Kroetsch, Laurence, and Ross certainly left. That is what I am saying in the last two lines of the poem "They have left the farm, / they are going somewhere." The somewhere my parents went was only thirty miles away from where they grew up, but they did leave. They went to the nearest small city but they left the desolation and isolation of farm life as they knew it.

Interviewers: Although you did not grow up on a farm, you keep writing about farms.

Crozier: I think I tend to mythologise the farm because I didn't grow up there. I grew up in what we called a "city," although there were only 15,000 people, but used to visit my grandparents' farm on Sundays. My grandmother would kill chickens and pluck them. I think my fascination with animals of all sorts is a city person's fascination. I don't have the practical view of animals that a person who has grown up on a farm has.

Interviewers: Do you have a more exotic view?

Crozier: Yes. I have a poem in my new manuscript about cleaning chickens. I remember when I'd show up on the farm on Sundays with my parents I'd ask my aunts if I could clean the chicken and pull out all the guts. And everyone would say, "Sure!" I couldn't understand why they didn't want to do it because I thought it was the most interesting thing. I thought people should fight over this privilege. For me it was fascinating to see the gravel in the gizzard, and the little transparent eggs that came out in a string and looked like moonstones. So, I had

the city person's fascination with the farm, occasionally, to fulfil those urban fantasies. It's interesting that some people think I grew up on a farm. The farm is never a real place for me — it is an imagined place. It's funny, when Patrick and I were first together we'd be driving through the country and Patrick would ask, "what's that crop over there?" I'd say, "That's Durham wheat," or "that's barley." About a year ago he asked me what something was and I said, "Pat, I haven't got a clue. All these years you've been asking me that and all I know are the names, *barley, rye* and *Durham wheat!*" (Laughter). He assumed because I'd grown up in Saskatchewan I knew the names of all these crops.

Interviewers: How did you meet Patrick Lane?

Crozier: I was teaching in Swift Current at the time, and he came to give a poetry workshop in Regina and I drove in for it. I was familiar with his work. Robert Currie gave me a copy of Patrick's book, *Beware the Months of Fire*, because he claimed that we both had a similar sensibility. I must admit that when I looked at the picture on the back of the book, I thought he was a fat old man. I went in with my poems, and we met each other and chemistry happened. He was living with a woman and had two kids, and I was married and we sort of drifted away and looked at each other out of the corners of our eyes. Then, two years later, we met again at a Saskatchewan Writer's Guild Conference. We saw each other's names on the programme and both of us knew something was going to happen. I knew I was going to meet one of my destinies, and he knew he was too! (Laughter.) About two months later we ran off together. He got in his car in British Columbia, picked me up in Saskatchewan, and we just buggered off. I wrote a note to my husband and said I'm on my way to Toronto with another poet and said goodbye. We went to Toronto and I met, for the first time, people like Al Purdy and Joe

Rosenblatt who had just been names in a book. We began our relationship by staying in Joe Rosenblatt's house in Toronto — a weird beginning!

Interviewers: How did No Longer Two People *come about?*

Crozier: Patrick and I had been together about two months and we were living in Winnipeg where he was the Writer-in-Residence. We had had an argument about something, and I wrote the first poem in the sequence and showed it to him. He said he wasn't going to let me get away with that and replied by writing a poem in response. Then we thought, this could be fun, why don't we just continue on and bounce one poem off another. We were both reading Jung at the time too. All that summer, on the way to Winnipeg from Toronto, we had been talking about male and female voices in poetry and wondering whether there was a difference or not. We had hoped the sequence would be mythological and personal and give us some answers to the question of voice and gender, but nobody read it that way. (Laughter.)

Interviewers: Could you comment on that? The critical reaction was overpoweringly negative.

Crozier: It was. It was 'how dare these people air their soiled sheets in public!' It surprised both of us. We had chosen the title *No Longer Two People* from a Picasso quote, in which he more or less said, these are no longer two people but forms, vibrations, and colours. People didn't realize that from the title. They thought we meant we were one person joined in holy unmatrimony.

Interviewers: So the title is meant to be read ironically.

Crozier: Yes. That's what we had hoped, but people took it at face value and didn't sense the irony. I remember after it came out we read it in Winnipeg, and someone came up to us afterwards and asked how we could stand in front of an audience and take our clothes off like that. The funny thing about the book is that it has come into its own again. Ten years after its publication, it's getting positive critical reactions from people like Fred Wah.

Interviewers: What people don't realize, possibly, is that there seems to be an argument going on between the two voices.

Crozier: Exactly! I think, in fact, if the poems have a problem it is that they are not personal enough. I don't think we'd write the same thing now. I think we'd be more risqué and daring.

Interviewers: What do you think you've learned from Patrick Lane?

Crozier: That's a hard one. How to boil a five minute egg? How to grow a vegetable garden? (Laughter). He's taught me a lot about craft, about how to structure a poem. I've always admired his integrity and his talent. And he has one of the eyes that I know of for finding what's good or bad about a poem.

Interviewers: Returning to what you were saying a minute ago about The Depression, we were walking along Queen's Park Crescent one day with Timothy Findley and the conversation shifted to the topic of the Depression and the Crash. His family had been well-to-do Torontonians and had been hit hard by the events of October '29. When one of us asked him what actually happened, he stopped and turned and the fire came into his eyes and he replied "It's not the sort of thing people sat around talking about!" The Depression and the Crash are almost missing events in Canadian literature.

Crozier: Well, except for Sinclair Ross, W.O. Mitchell, or Margaret Laurence in *The Stone Angel.*

Interviewers: And Hugh MacLennan and Barry Broadfoot.

Crozier: Yes. Sinclair Ross was central to me and my literary imagination because his stories were the first things I read and identified with. His stories were like my parent's' stories and I'd never seen those books before. It was the first thing I read that I could really understand as my own. Ross lived for some time in southwest Saskatchewan where I'm from. The wind he wrote about is the same wind. The false fronts on the stores and the closed nature of small-town society were things I could identify with. These were things I saw everyday around me and seeing those things in a "work of literature" made me realize that I could be a writer. It was the same with Margaret Laurence. It is interesting that a generation apart, the same book was the signal work for us, perhaps because the Depression is such a central myth in the West. And unlike Findley's family, mine talked about the Thirties all the time. As you say, considering its importance, it hasn't really worked its way into the writing as much as one would think, especially in Eastern Canada.

Interviewers: Is it because the Depression is almost an issue too painful to confront, in comparison to other issues in our history?

Crozier: Well, it affected Saskatchewan more than any other province because we had the drought along with the stock market crash. Right now, history seems to be repeating itself because we're in the middle of another drought and another slump. Everyone in Saskatchewan has embedded in them that fear of the drought and of the Depression, and the knowledge that it is coming again.

Interviewers: In the interview you gave to Doris Hillis in Voices and Visions, *you said poetry was an "out" for you, "a way of escaping from the kind of life you saw around you." Could you elaborate?*

Crozier: I'm the only person from my family who has ever gone to university, and that includes a long line of cousins. Who was it who said that the two ways of getting out of the lower class are either through sports or art? I think it was Hugh Garner. Definitely, I'm a working class kid from a working class background. Writing to escape wasn't a conscious decision, but it was a way to enter a world I knew nothing about — it had nothing to do with the world I came from. My parents' house wasn't full of books and we certainly did not discuss literature. Patrick asks, "Did you read Winnie the Pooh as a kid?" and I say "No," and he asks if I read this or that when I was small, I say no again, and he looks shocked. I really don't know why, given that background, writing became something I wanted to do. I remember going to my first library. I thought I had discovered a gold mine, partly because I had been deprived of books during my early years. Poetry is something my family doesn't understand, although they don't feel any antipathy toward it. I don't think my father has read anything I've ever written. In fact, he doesn't read at all, except for the *Swift Current Sun*. My mom is proud of me; she doesn't understand why I write or what the poems mean, but my books are on the coffee table. And I think she enjoys seeing herself in some of the poems — or at least my version of her.

Interviewers: Do you feel you bring anything from that working-class background that has been positive for your poetry?

Crozier: I hope so. The voice in poems like "The Women Who Survive", or "My Aunt's Ghost", is the voice of a small-town, Saskatchewan working woman. The colloquial expressions are definitely from families like mine. And I hope I'm introducing a content into poetry that comes out of my particular place in the world — Western, female, working-class. Collectively, these qualities have not been that prevalent in our literature.

Interviewers: Do you feel it has given you more freedom with language?

Crozier: I don't know if it has given me more freedom, but I think it has probably made me use language differently.

Interviewers: Do you feel that there is a solid tradition of working class writing in Canada with writers like Al Purdy, Joe Wallace, and Milton Acorn?

Crozier: Yeah, but it is male, isn't it? Al Purdy, Alden Nowlan, Joe Rosenblatt, Milton Acorn, and definitely Patrick [Lane]. I can't think of any women from Purdy's and Nowlan's generation.

Interviewers: Well, what about Livesay, or is she pretend working-class?

Crozier: I think her worst poems are her working-class poems. Her best are her lyrics, her love poems. Her Thirties poems about the working-class of the dispossessed like *Day and Night* and *Call My People Home* just don't work for me. But her poems about being a woman, about aging, and loving, do. Pat Lowther is probably the first Canadian woman to write out of the kind of world I come from. And others like Bronwen Wallace are writing about it with insight and honesty.

Interviewers: A number of Saskatchewan writers, when they write about what they know, inevitably have to come to terms with the fact of the Prairie. For example, Eli Mandel transforms the Prairie through his "döppleganger" metaphor for being "out of place." W.O. Mitchell treats it as a metaphor for the eternal in Who Has Seen the Wind.

Crozier: One thing I've never done is write about "the Prairie." I wouldn't say any of my poems are about "the Prairie." In most of my poems I use the images that surround me, and that includes the Prairie, but the poems are *about* something else like love or death or growing old. In the poems about my parents I include the particular details of the place because that's where they came from.

Interviewers: Ed Dyck, in his article in NeWest Review, *notes that your "mastery of the Prairie metaphor has very little to do with the regionalism of its vehicle."*

Crozier: Dyck's implication is that the Prairie images and metaphors are in the poems because they are outside the poems. They are there in my life. If I lived near the ocean, I might have more sea imagery in my poetry. As it is, I can't write about the ocean in the same way that I write about my environment. I don't know that landscape. I look on the ocean as a tourist. I can only write about it as a tourist. Consciously, I don't think about the Prairie. It is something that is in my blood and in my bones; it's home. I don't say, "My god, look at all this space — I must write about it!"

Interviewers: And all that Durham wheat too! (Laughter).

Crozier: Yeah! Exactly. It's never something that consciously enters my mind. It is just where I am at home. My poems come out of other things. They come out of my reaction, my emotional response to what is going on in the world.

Interviewers: So the poems come from inside rather than outside you.

Crozier: Both, but the outside is always filtered through my way of seeing things. I believe the landscape in my poems is more an internal landscape than an external one.

Interviewers: That's interesting because a lot of the poets who have emerged since 1970 are writing from that internal world rather than the old external world of writers such as Pratt, for example. Bronwen Wallace, for instance, is writing about, and from, a much more internal landscape, what is going on inside her memories and her thoughts.

Crozier: Yes, inside them, and the narrative of the place, the people, and the politics rather than the landscape itself.

Interviewers: Do you think it comes down to the fact that we've settled the landscape and now we're trying to figure out what's going on inside our own heads — trying to articulate the inner experience?

Crozier: Definitely, but also, unlike Eli Mandel who left the Prairies, I've never felt out of place here. Whenever I've read criticism of Prairie literature, I'm always amazed at the assertion that it is a hostile landscape. I've always felt at home here. I do not view the landscape as barren and overwhelming. I view it as very beautiful and comfortable. The landscape may seem shocking to others and they may feel out of place, but I don't.

Interviewers: Dyck claims that the Prairie tends to emphasize the human figure more than the landscape itself because the human figure stands out like an exclamation mark.

Crozier: Does anyone write about the landscape in isolation anymore? I think we're beyond the new land, new language thing of our earlier literature. The fact is, we have a literature we can all feed off now, and there is no reason to keep defining the "land". We've defined and ordered it to death. Now, as writers, we have to rediscover the spiritual and magical in it. We have to save it. Our old definitions of "landscape" and the way we live in it don't work.

Interviewers: You don't see yourself as a regional writer.

Crozier: No. I get quite annoyed at that phrase because I think Toronto is a region as well, although no one calls it that. I think my writing comes out of the Prairies. A meadowlark may find its way into my poems, but it is more than just a meadowlark. In the introduction to *The New Canadian Poets*, Dennis Lee identified a Prairie school of writing which he did not put me in. He had an asterisk beside my name and noted that I had written poems which could belong to this school, but that he had chosen not to include any. He chose others. I'm not even sure what this "school" is because I think the West's best writers are individual and idiosyncratic. They don't write like anyone else.

Interviewers: Dyck also mentions something called "The Moose Jaw Movement." What was that?

Crozier: (Laughter). This goes way way back to about 1974 or so. Robert Currie...

Interviewers: Who was editor of Salt...

Crozier: ...and one of the publishers of Coteau Books. He and I met at Fort San Summer School of the Arts. We showed each other our poems and we had so much fun criticising each other's writing we thought we'd like this to go on. When he went back to Moose Jaw, he found Gary Hyland, Ralph Ring, Jim McLean and Ed Dyck (who was still living there then and teaching math). Byrna Barclay and Judy Krause came from Regina, and I drove in from Swift Current where I was teaching high school. We'd meet in Moose Jaw once a month with poems and more than one case of beer. Robert Kroetsch was in town once and he helped us come up with the name for our group. The statement we were trying to make was "hey folks, good poetry can even come out of Moose Jaw." Moose Jaw is the great joke of Canada, right? The group, though the faces have changed, still meets.

Interviewers: Since 1975, you've published seven books of poetry. Your work seems to have gone through several phases. There are more twists of thought and more of a playfulness in the diction, and more puns. What are the most marked changes that you see in your work?

Crozier: You summed it up very well. I think I was an extremely passionate, strident writer when I began. I had a bottle full of feelings just waiting for an outlet. I'm embarrassed by a lot of those poems now when I look at them. They are very angry, very serious poems. I took myself too seriously then.

Interviewers: There are no poems like "The Sex Lives of Vegetables."

Crozier: No, I wouldn't have been able to write poems like those back then. I think I have just loosened up. (Laughter). Thank God. I still have a lot of anger that has to come out, but in more subtle ways I hope. And over the past ten years I think I've learned a lot about diction and tone. And I've extended the range of what I write about and varied the form.

Interviewers: Such as?

Crozier: I think I would never have written a poem in sequence in the early years. I've become more and more interested in taking more than one look at something. "The Foetus Dreams" is an example where I give ten views of the foetus' dreaming. I think that is more of a post-modern view, where one tries approaching something from ten different angles and directions, from left and right and upside-down. Where does that come from? I don't know. I don't know why that developed; whether it is just maturity as a writer or as a person, I'm not sure. It just may be that I'm a much happier person now. I'm in a very happy relationship and I'm more self-confident. I think that self-confidence allows you to take more risks and to extend yourself, to try different things. For example, to be playful about sex or to be irreverent about sex is still a risky thing to do, especially if you are a woman writer. I've had people walk out of my readings — someone at Scarborough College a couple of years ago got up and left in the middle of my reading "The Sex Lives of Vegetables." I still get the occasional "hate letter" in the mail. There are still certain words that carry a powerful punch that some people don't believe belong in poems, especially poems written by a woman. It doesn't bother me anymore, well, not as much anyway, if I upset people, if I challenge them. I think you have to if you want to write well.

Interviewers: There's an aggressive tone and a playful tone about sex in some of the poems that one usually only finds in poems written by males.

Crozier: Yes. Some critics still think it isn't a woman's place to use that stance or that language.

Interviewers: Did you mean to shock people with them?

Crozier: No. The first time I read the vegetable poems I didn't think they'd be shocking. I thought they'd just be fun. Initially, I wondered if they were even too silly to be published because it seems to me we've been trained to take poetry very seriously. We tend to think if we laugh at a poem, it's somehow a lesser poem. And in our country, even in the 80's, if a woman writes humorously about sex, she's morally suspect, and her poems will upset a number of people who read them. I've written a new sequence now that I know is going to be shocking to some people, although again, that was not my intent. I've written a series of penis poems. Patrick said penises should be poked fun at. All the same, I needed his assurances that I wasn't going completely off my rocker, that I was doing something that was valid.

Interviewers: *While we're on the topic of sex, one theme that keeps turning up in your work is that of Leda and the Swan. It is in "Pavlova" and "Forms of Innocence." Why do you keep returning to that?*

Crozier: I come back to it in the penis sequence too, in a poem called "Penis/Bird." The myth itself is an extremely powerful one, isn't it? A woman being raped by a big bird is both ridiculous and powerful at the same time. It really twists your imagination trying to figure out exactly what happened during this encounter. And also, no matter what other meanings we read into it, the myth is about rape. Every woman grows up with the fear of rape. You can't stand at a bus depot or walk a street or cross a park anywhere across Canada without worrying about what the guy across the street is about to do. That's part of the female psyche — that fear of rape. Then, there's Yeats' brilliant poem about Leda and the Swan. It's the one I've read for years and I think it is a *tour de force*, an almost perfect poem, though as a woman reader I have difficulty with Leda's surrender. So you've got both the myth and the literary response to the myth, and then there's the very real fear every woman has of rape, another reason for the driving force behind that ancient story.

Interviewers: *So you're not concerned with the rape of Leda as the indirect cause of the Trojan war, as in Yeats' poem.*

Crozier: No, I've tried to bring it down to a more common, personal level in my poem. In "Forms of Innocence," I've changed the incident from an act of rape to an act of lovemaking, and have located it in the backseat of a car on the Prairies beside a stubble field, into the context of where I come from.

Interviewers: *Dreams are another important theme in your work, the striving for another alternative reality.*

Crozier: Oh, definitely. I'm a person who is very affected by my dreams. I have dreamt that Patrick has had an affair and I've gotten out of bed and not spoken to him the whole day. (Laughter).

Interviewers: *They're that real?*

Crozier: How do you tell the difference between dream and reality? For instance, at one point Patrick and I and some friends were sitting around the dinner table and we were just having an interesting conversation about our first memories. I said that my first memory was a very vivid one. I was about four and my family was living in an old house that had a dirt cellar. My mother sent me down to the cellar to get a jar of pickles. When I was down there, I saw this huge lizard on the floor. I called my mother and she came running downstairs with a butcher knife, stabbed the lizard in the back, and opened the furnace door and threw it in. That's probably where I get my view of strong women from. I remember saying this to Patrick and he looked at me and said, "It wouldn't have been a lizard. You don't have lizards on the Prairie." I said no, it was a lizard and it was about a foot long. We argued and he said it must have been a salamander. He suggested I phone my mother and ask her. So I phoned her, reminded her of the incident, and asked her whether it was a salamander or a lizard. She had no idea what I was talking about and told me I must have been dreaming, that it never happened! What I carried around in my head as my first memory was probably a dream. How do you know the difference between things that happen and things that don't but that you have memories of anyway? I think that first memory of mine has shaped the way I see the world, has shaped my way of viewing my mother and women in general. A lot of my poems come from that first powerful memory. You get into that whole subconscious idea of the dirt cellar and the mythical beast. So my dreams are as important as other aspects of my life. They're as real.

Interviewers: *So that would allow you to make that very imaginative leap to write something like "The Foetus Dreams."*

Crozier: The genesis of that poem came from an article I read. A scientist, using electrodes placed on the outside of a woman's belly actually picked up the brain waves of a foetus while it was still inside the mother, and he claimed that those brain waves signified that the foetus was dreaming. I found that fascinating. What do you dream before you actually see anything or experience anything? How do you dream a *tree* before you've seen a tree? What faces do you dream? In order to answer that I had to flip into Jungian psychology and the collective unconscious.

Interviewers: *Robert Bly has a theory about the different types of brains — the reptile brain, the mammal brain, and the higher more developed type of brain that dreams in geometric shapes.*

Crozier: Well, I've got a salamander or lizard brain! (Laughter).

Interviewers: *You've written two very strong poems about abortion, "A Poem About Nothing" and "The Foetus Dreams." There is a real sympathy in those poems for the situation of the foetus...*

Crozier: I'm very interested in prenatal life — in what goes on in the womb, in what face we wear inside our mothers, in what we become, and what we leave behind at birth. But I think the worst thing that could possibly happen would be if someone from the Pro-life side used "The Foetus Dreams" or any of my other poems that explore this kind of thing to say that there should be no abortions. It would be horrible because I definitely am on the pro-choice side. I am also "Pro-life". That

term is one of the biggest misnomers because, of course, pro-choice people also believe in life; they are *for* life. I definitely believe a woman should make the decision about whether she should have an abortion. The lines in "A Poem About Nothing," the ones about the girl jumping three stories to abort, should suggest the terrible acts women are driven to when they cannot get a safe, legal, inexpensive abortion.

Interviewers: *In the last section of* The Garden Going on Without Us, *entitled "What the Mind Turns Over" you write a series of biographical poems about historical figures — Nijinsky, Pavlova, Gorky. What attracted you to those characters?*

Crozier: It's funny they're all Russian. That was purely coincidental. It happened to be what I was reading at the time. I love Nijinsky's diary — it's got to be one of the most passionate diaries ever written. I picked up Gorky's My Childhood in a second-hand bookstore and read it one afternoon. The tale grabbed hold of me. Again, it has all kinds of feministic implications, of men being the owners of language. Even though Gorky's grandmother actually talked out loud to angels, it was the grandfather who could read and write and, therefore, only he knew the actual words needed to talk to angels and to God. So it was just that I was reading about those lives and they had some connection with what I was thinking and feeling at the time. The "Pavlova" poem really started when I was twelve years old and I saw a clip of her on the *Ed Sullivan Show*. She was doing the dance of the dying swan from *Swan Lake*. I thought it was one of the most beautiful things I had ever seen, in fact it was the first and only ballet I saw as a child in small-town Saskatchewan. For me, Pavlova epitomised the ultimate in feminine grace and beauty. Then, when I was in my twenties, I read an article in a magazine written by Pavlova's travelling secretary, and she spoke about what Pavlova's life and death had really been like. That image of beauty just went bang! She died of tuberculosis or pneumonia, lonely and homesick, in a foreign country with an unloving husband at her bedside. The merging of the film clip and the article were what produced the poem.

Interviewers: What are the challenges of living in a two-poet household?

Crozier: For one thing, when you live with another poet there's an understanding of why you have to write. My husband didn't understand that compulsion. Most of the poems I was working on at the time he found extremely threatening, probably rightly so. But when you live with another poet, he understands that there's a need to write about the dark things as well as the bright and happy. And he understands that poetry isn't my whole life either. It's only a part, but it's an important part that helps to make up what I am, the good and the bad of it. It's hard for someone who doesn't write to understand that.

Interviewers: Yes, that's like what you say in the poem "A Conclusion", "there is nothing better / than poetry". What would be better than poetry?

Crozier: I'm not going to answer that! (Laughter).

Two Windows:

The road to North Hatley from Montreal winds through the flat dairy lands of the Eastern Townships, past the Monteregion Hills and south toward Sherbrooke and the American border. When we arrived in Sherbrooke we walked over to a taxi and asked for a ride for the last fourteen miles of our journey, beyond Lennoxville, to the resort town on Lake Massawippi. The driver looked blankly at us. Again we asked, this time in French. Nothing registered. Another driver stepped up. "It's not that he won't speak to you because you are Anglais — he's deaf and can only lip-read in Quebecois French."

North Hatley, a bilingual town settled by the English and populated by the French, exists within that linguistic and geographical tension that has come to symbolise the contemporary Quebec. Situated about ten miles inside Quebec from Vermont (you can see the hills of Vermont on a clear day), the town was the summer home of numerous writers — Hugh MacLennan, F.R. Scott, to name a few. Ralph Gustafson and Ron Sutherland make their permanent homes there. Louis Dudek lives nearby. As if the town is not Canadianised enough by virtue of being our own version of Concord — a gathering place for a generation of writers — it is also the former summer home of Montreal Canadiens Manager Sam Pollock.

Although North Hatley may seem a bastion for Anglo-Canada, a place fortified by the presence of literary talent, it became, paradoxically, a centre of debate in the Separation Referendum of 1989 and voted overwhelmingly "Oui". As a place not only in contemporary Canadian literature but also Canadian politics, North Hatley is a curious blend of the tensions that are reflected throughout Quebec and Canada. It is also the place where D.G. Jones has chosen to live and write, and his work, like the town and country, survives and matures, not only despite the tensions, but because of them.

Born in Bancroft Ontario in 1929 and educated at McGill, D.G. Jones is the author of *The Sun is Axeman* (1961), *Phrases from Orpheus* (1967), *Under the Thunder the Flowers Light Up the Earth* (1977, for which he won the Governor General's Award for Poetry), *A Throw of Particles* (1983), and *Balthazar and Other Poems* (1988). He is also author of the critical study of Canadian literature, *Butterfly on Rock* (1970). He teaches at the Université de Sherbrooke.

We conducted this interview, May 25, 1985 in Jones' living room at North Hatley. There are two windows in that room. One faces onto the garden at the side of the house where a myriad of flowers blooms in a wild disorder. The other window looks across Lake Massawippi onto the rugged forests of southern Quebec and the faint blue hills of Vermont.

Interviewers: North Hatley seems to be quite the place for writers to live.

Jones: The attraction of the place is the lake and the village, and in a sense, the scenery. It's a good place to live in the summer. You can swim in the lake. The population then swells to two or three times its normal size, but in the winter it is just a very small village and there's hardly anyone here. Hugh MacLennan once met me in the post office and complained that there were getting to be too many people living here all the time. I wasn't sure if he was telling me I should move out or what. I don't know if he was aware of the fact that I was living here all the time. F.R. Scott lived over just a few streets and up the hill. Scott had the place here for twenty or more years. We only saw him about once a year. He had his birthday party every summer, and would invite a number of people; Louis Dudek, A.J.M. Smith, Buffy (John) Glassco, Ralph Gustafson, Ron Sutherland, and myself, and some of his other friends from the village. We'd all meet at least once a year on his veranda overlooking the lake. Those were memorable parties.

Interviewers: Do all of you here view this as a literary centre? Does this help or hinder your work?

Jones: Well, it's partly a myth that it helps literary work. North Hatley is not a creative centre in the sense of a lot of people getting together and stimulating each other. We don't do things together, at all, as a rule. I hear Ralph's piano more than I see him. I see Louis Dudek, who has a place in Ways Mills about twenty-five miles from here, maybe only a couple of times a year in the summer. The other people — MacLennan and Scott — we'd see once or twice a summer depending on the year and their health. Most people live more or less independently. Hugh MacLennan up the hill rarely comes here now. Frank Scott, A.J.M. Smith and Buffy (John) Glassco are all dead now. In the last four or five years that whole generation has disappeared. These were the people who used to get together and share their ideas and friendships more often. When Frank was well he used to have picnics up the lake at his squatter's cabin that his brother built.

Interviewers: You turn up in the NFB film on Frank Scott at one of his birthday parties.

Jones: Yeah. We go back a few years to the days of the Kewatin Conference. My first wife, Kim Ondaatje, invited a few of the people there up to the cottage. That was while I was still in Ontario. We had one or two birthday parties for him up there in the Fifties. Then he started having his parties here. It was a nice tradition. I wouldn't say, in general, that there is a North Hatley aesthetic as such. People came here at different times for different reasons. Gustafson came here because he was born nearby in Sherbrooke. I came here because, when I left Bishops' University for the University of Sherbrooke, Ron Sutherland told me that there was a house for sale next door to him. It was partly accident and partly the attraction of the area that led us here, and it has been very pleasant here for a number of years. Glassco, who was over in Knowlton, used to come by in his little yellow roadster. He'd drive around looking very sporty in his tweed-jacket, driving cap, and white moustache. He looked like something that just stepped out of the Edwardian era or the nineteen twenties. He was a peculiar figure coming to what is, in many ways, a peculiar village. Almost from the beginning, North Hatley was a tourist place but mainly for Americans. It then became more and more Canadian, predominantly Anglophone, and has now become partly Francophone. In a sense, the town's whole fate was beginning to be worked out at the time the Arabs started buying out the area a few years back. A kind of proper vengeance. But in a way too, in the early days the town attracted Americans who were writers or academics. A man named Hughes, who wrote one of the first sociological studies of French Canada, had a cottage up here in his later years. Mason Wade was here for a while when he was working on a book on French Canada. I suppose there *was* a climate, to some degree, that was created here by various writers, some of them academics. It is not entirely accident, I suppose.

Interviewers: North Hatley turns up as a place in a number of people's poems. E.D. Blodgett tries to make something out of this in his introduction to A Throw of Particles. *He claims that "place" is the beginning of consciousness. How important is place in poetry?*

Jones: That depends a great deal on the poet. It is a nice question: to what extent do you have to be rooted in a place? I suspect that one of the people who thought place very important was D.H. Lawrence yet he moved all over the world, which suggests a slight paradox or complication in any argument of this sort. Joyce, of course, ended up writing about one place wherever the hell he was, so much so, that it became a place in his mind. But it seems to me that on the other hand, for English Canadian writers, at least, there is a

tremendous investment in space, and most Canadian poetry is highly spatial. If I can make a distinction between French and English Canadian writing, it seems to me that with English Canada the concern is with control over space, and with French Canada the concern is over time. The French Canadians want to preserve a past which is verbal, symbolic, and historic, but space tends often to be ignored or to disappear for about a hundred years in some of their more important poets. For many of French Canada's poets, space is almost meaningless up to a certain point because it is an ideal world that they are trying to cultivate and they can't; whereas in English Canada the poets and the people are always trying to organize space into something, or along some civil lines as in Dennis Lee's *Civil Elegies*. They began with some considerable optimism doing that — they cut down the trees and put up the houses and the roads with the hope that as the village grows it will turn into a beautiful garden city. Often, it was a completely different kind of economic activity at work in English Canada. They created temporary lumber towns and mining towns which weren't garden cities in the least. This is the great argument, to some degree, in English Canadian poetry. But in Quebec, space is largely a prison, and they try to escape from it through all kinds of imaginative and verbal games. As far as the most extreme or intense expression of this goes in novels such as those by Acquin or Ducharme, space is not something which is manageable, and it is not manageable because they don't control the physical and economic apparatus that would allow them to hold onto or to develop the space on their own terms. More profoundly in the poets, they aren't interested in the space anyway, but in some kind of ideal world. Space becomes a meaningless entity, an expanse, because it is merely accidental, temporal, and ephemeral. They are pursuing some kind of absolute which they can't find; St. Denys Garneau, Emile Nelligan, Alain

Grandbois. In those poets, the details of space just disappear. French Canadian poets don't write about the backyard and they don't write about all the different kinds of trees or the kinds of particulars that you find in Lampman, Purdy, Souster, or Birney.

Interviewers: Or in your own poetry, for instance.

Jones: Well, in that respect, you see, I'm more or less a typical Canadian, especially throughout the earlier poetry. A poem usually begins anchored in some particular space. It is not as obvious as it is in the work of someone like Souster or Birney where you can tell exactly where the poet is, you can tell what street-corner in Toronto or Montreal the poet is standing on. He'll tell you everything about the local area, the time of day, which day of the week it is.

Interviewers: You talk about the French Canadian writers and their desire to control the apparatus of their economic environment. Do you think that was at the root of the Separatist movement?

Jones: I'm not sure, but that was a very real aspect of it. For a hundred years or so they let the English have all the commerce and they looked after the spiritual world. But the spiritual world was something elsewhere. The revolution said "we're going to take charge of our own world," which meant they were going to take charge of their own space and the physical and material things that go with it. But even still, you don't get the kind of detail, the kind of realistic cataloguing of local space that you find in English Canadian poetry. From the point of view of traditional French Canadian aesthetics English poetry is not poetry but just prose.

Interviewers: What was it like to live here during the 1980 Referendum on Separatism?

Jones: There was certainly a lot of publicity about North Hatley. There was a fair amount of stirring. Jacquie, the lady who runs the patisserie here organized Sunday brunches for everybody. She had Australian TV and Quebec TV and I don't know how many different TV crews were here. But during the brunches she was the centre of media exposure. Her concern was to raise the level of activity. She was a good "PQiste" herself. She was getting people from all over to come to North Hatley to discuss the Referendum. It worked in a way. It certainly made the place a little more lively. I voted PQ and so did my wife. But for my next door neighbour, there was no way he was going to vote PQ, and he told me I was nuts, that I was crazy. Maybe I was, maybe I wasn't. On the whole it was a good thing. It certainly changed the temper of Quebec. Good for Quebec in general, but bad for the PQ in that people discovered that they could separate if they really wanted to, but now it's not so urgent.

Interviewers: How, specifically, was the Referendum good for Quebec? All we really hear about in English Canada are the negative aspects for the English-speaking Quebequers like yourself.

Jones: As to the business moving out of Quebec, there's been a lot about that but I think that just coincided with 'capital west' — the movement of businesses west in general. I suppose the two together were somewhat devastating. As far as relationships between French and English in the province are concerned and the general state of mind of most Quebecois, it has been highly valuable and positive. It has put the English-speaking Quebequers on the defensive and they are more obviously a minority now. They have also begun to learn French in a way that they didn't before. For the French-speaking Quebecois, it has been profoundly good, psychologically. It made them feel at home in their own province, and it also made them feel that, at least in part, they were worthy enough to make their own decisions and that they don't have to feel totally intimidated or like an inferior group in the population. It has meant a certain real development in terms of Quebequers getting into industry, business, and technology, partly because of the vacuum created by 'capital west' and partly because of the new emphasis on education and a desire to participate in taking charge of their society. In that respect it has worked very well.

Interviewers: As a University teacher, you may have noticed that there has been an entirely new generation since the Quiet Revolution who have no notion of what Quebec was like before. Has Quebec developed a sort of cultural amnesia about its past?

Jones: In a very general way, yes. One is aware of this. It is like asking students "what happened in the Second World War?" Most of them don't know. To talk about "la grande noir-sûr," that real isolation and depression that one saw and felt under Duplesis among writers at that time is to present a statement of historical affairs that doesn't register with the young people. It is a world. It's a phrase you can put some meaning to, but it is an experience they don't know anything about. I'm not sure, in a very general sense, that many of them are aware of their poetry, their novels, and the literature, or the cultural battles that went on. That's probably an aspect of the general educational system, and perhaps of young people across the continent. There's not as much, even, of a political awareness as there used to be. Many of the young people would just as soon have jobs as worry about the Constitution. A lot of them are part of a popular culture which is not terribly interested in rationalism.

Interviewers: You use both French and English in your poems. What point are you trying to make by dropping French phrases into English poems and vice versa?

Jones: I'm not trying to make a political point. It is more of an artistic indulgence on my part. Even though I'm not very good at languages, and I don't know my French that well, the words in other languages are like different coloured building blocks you can use in writing. I use them partly because of the colouring, the tone, the rhythm, the nuance — something that you can get with these other words. It is a kind of gymnastics too. It depends on the poem. It is used more in the spirit of a game than for any kind of political message. Even when there is a kind of political message — I wrote a poem "I Annihilate" which goes on to try and suggest that in the colour of a purple finch in the snow there is a variety of different images which run into the French "c'est un tache sur la page blanche." Then the next phrase "une cauchemar en rose" is a contradiction in terms. It goes on to "le Quebec libre" which I thought was a nice idea so I put it in — it is not really a statement for the liberty of Quebec one way or the other but rather a lyrical version of politics. Basically, French and English are the same language. They share much of the common vocabulary — forty to sixty percent of each language is shared. It is hard, however, to operate in both languages, although my wife Monique does it as do many people around here.

Interviewers: Your early poems are more concerned with images of nature while your later work seems more preoccupied with human images. Was this shift between the two conscious?

Jones: Not really, but one tries, in part, every now and then to write about something else. The 'Lampman poems' are in many ways nature poems, but they are given a dramatic setting and a narrative motif which helps to prevent them from being descriptive poems or nature poems — whatever you want to call them. On the other hand, there is an interest in people in the later poems and a little bit more community. I've spent most of my life living in an isolated way. I've never really lived in a large city. North Hatley is isolated, especially in the winter; something which is attractive physically but not socially. This is a bit rough, but in the choice between the city and here, I've opted to stay here. Generally, in Quebec, I've felt more at home even though I've been a kind of outsider. Living in Guelph, even though there was no linguistic problem, I felt as much or more isolated there as I do here now.

Interviewers: There seems to be three poetries in Quebec: the Francophone; the Montreal urban-English poetry; and quite recently a non-Montreal English poetry.

Jones: Generally speaking, English poetry in Quebec has been a mixture of the urban and the pastoral. Frank Scott is an extremely urban man in many ways. Many of his more satirical poems are urban in their wit and often in their ambiance. But at the same time, he could write about the rocks and streams and trees he knew down here. Even more pronounced was the same sort of split in Buffy Glassco with his Parisian and Bohemian connection on the one hand, and the sort of rural postman of the eastern townships going down through Lucy's notch, meditating on decayed buildings—a mixture of Wordsworth and T.S. Eliot, which is really "Place Beau Brummel." It seems to me this is a curious kind of thread to find in this English Canadian poetry. Many of the poems Ralph Gustafson has been writing lately have been centred in and around North Hatley. They are partly about the local scene, but at the same time a lot of his poetry is about the whole rest of the world he's been travelling around for years. A lot of his poems are elliptical and rather learned. So he too is that kind of a mixture.

Interviewers: During the Sixties you took up the whole question of our "identity" in literature and through literature in your book Butterfly on Rock. *Do you think we've gotten over our anxieties about who we are and what we are?*

Jones: You should write whatever you write and then the identity emerges from that. It seems inevitable that you are going to be caught in the existing identity when you begin, which is perfectly normal. Prairie writers never really wrote any poetry until about 1970. But they helped found the Canadian novel. There were really no poets out there, and all of a sudden in the 70's they started writing poetry. What they wrote was very much like any other kind of English Canadian poetry. Everybody was talking about his local place, everybody was trying to catalogue his meaning, his prairie world and his grandfather and his mother. It sounded like English Canadian poetry all over again. In a way it was a little tired because although it sounded new to them we'd heard it before: it was realistic, documentary, descriptive and discursive. It seemed to me that they were saying that they had an authentic and different prairie culture. But they didn't produce a poetry that was all that different from the poetry of eastern Canada.

Interviewers: Is that what you meant when you said in your essay "Grounds for Translation," that "the common language shared by English Canadians and Americans provided an illusion of a common identity." There doesn't seem to be the kind of discoveries that you mentioned in the essay — such as Lee's discovery of St. Denys Garneau — going on today. This discovery by Lee led to his realisation of the common bonds between English and French Canadians.

Jones: We've been defined, partly, by the way we've reacted to the United States. Part of the definition of Canada has been its peculiar, cautious, and ambiguous attitude towards the United States. We defined ourselves, partly by living here, partly by rejecting the States, a cultivation of the more conservative aspects of British culture. By and large, from what I've seen in English Canadian literature, we've arrived at what Margaret Atwood might call a "schizophrenia." With the exception of E.J. Pratt, we've written poems and novels for a century and a half that are informed by the idea for a pastoral longing for a settled land. And yet our whole economy is in absolute contradiction to it. The real power and the real wealth is wielded by this, and by and large, not articulate in the literature. For instance, French Canada was viewed as a great intellectual and spiritual centre. But when you look in the literature for the great spiritual and philosophical and theological works you don't find them. There wasn't a hell of a lot there, and meanwhile the rest of the population is out cursing everybody and going to the States to work in the cotton mills. The literature kept saying to them "we are a great agricultural nation," but the reality was that there was just a bit of good land along the rivers that couldn't support the bulk of the population and the rest of the country was just rock! A lot of people were living there with that image of themselves and their world. Whereas, the reality is often quite different. English Canadians, also, keep thinking in terms of having their garden and their house and their family, and yet half of them keep wandering back and forth across Canada to find a job to keep their house in the Maritimes safe. And the jobs they find are not meant to create any kind of settled pastoral world at all.

Interviewers: It is interesting that you make that distinction because the three images that come up most often in your poetry are the garden, the flower and the thunder.

Jones: I suppose there is a point in my work where I said to myself that the garden is a serious image. When I think about gardens I can see a certain Canadian dream and I can see that it makes sense. There were times in the late Sixties here when I could look out my window and see a Krieghoff type of landscape, very pastoral, and at the same time, have my TV on and watch all the stuff from Vietnam, the riots, and burning people, and the rocks being thrown; Detroit, Selma Alabama, the Israeli war. I'd look through one window and have one version of the world. It seemed to me that together they made up a somewhat jarring image of the world we live in and in a sense where we want to go and how we want to live. It is a metaphysical reality you see. Most English Canadian poets approach this reality through their relationship to their immediate natural surroundings. If there is a divinity it is mediated through the particulars of place, whether it is Lampman or Carman, or Scott. When English Canadians look for something profound or permanent they go to the rocks. F.R. Scott talks about digging in his garden in Westmount and finds the old shale below. Or Al Purdy talks about digging down through the layers and finding his past. The spirit is in the rock. There is something mystical about the Precambrian shield. Unfortunately, there is Precambrian rock in Africa and Australia. (Laughter). It is not totally Canadian. I guess God is not totally Canadian. (Laughter). There is a sense, in a great many Canadian poets, of an abandoned orthodox doctrinal religion — there are a lot of ministers' sons in there or people who are ministers: Frye and Pratt are ministers and Scott was a minister's son. They tend to approach anything fundamental through the landscape. Whether or not this connects to the fact that the first Canadian art gallery was on top of the Department of Mines and Surveys building in Ottawa, I don't know (Laughter).

Interviewers: In the poem "A Protestant Hymn" which is for Ralph Gustafson you call God an impossible God. Is that because we live in an impossible place?

Jones: God is impossible because you can't make absolute sense out of Him. If you try to make any definition of God, logical and doctrinal, it becomes impossible. If there is any religious framework at all for me it is in the Taoist sense. But when the Taoists start swallowing their own sperm to become immortal it is no different than any other rituals of established religion, and that's not for me.

Interviewers: What is it that attracts you to eastern religions?

Jones: The awareness of the non-human world and the cultivation of that world that you find in much of Chinese art and writing, and the slightly more immediate critical sense, too, that you find in the Taoists that is something very close to Derrida's position with regard to language that all of our language is relative and most of our concepts are a kind of a coded convention. The other thing that attracts me to it is their concept that what is reality is innumerable. I'm also attracted to their general attitude to rocks, plants, flowers, mountains, the world out there — this is the immediate non-human world I find enormously refreshing. Our own world is becoming increasingly a kind of concrete solipsism. Therefore, one has to find a way in which one can live in this world that is satisfying — the idea that one can just be in the world and have some kind of fruitful relationship with it, and that one can escape from one's limited self through something larger than oneself through getting to know the 'other,' which in many cases is more easily approached when it is more visibly non-human; plants, rocks, trees.

Interviewers: You've said a great deal in the past about what the Canadian poetic perception has been. What do you think it will be?

Jones: Well, I've always seen Canadian poetry as having a problem because even its pastoral dream is somewhat defeated by its highly spatial, highly realistic documentary general poetic. In a certain sense, it seemed to me that in the late Fifties and early Sixties, the so-called myth makers — Louis Dudek and Irving Layton presumably — (Layton is as close to Northrop Frye as anybody) they were trying to move Canadian poets away from the bias towards social realism, whereas the people who were working with Frye, such as Jay Macpherson, Reaney, or even people like Gwendolyn MacEwen and P.K. Page, were attempting to get English Canadian poetry off the ground or away from the documentary realistic school.

Interviewers: So where do we go from there?

Jones: That depends on where we find the writers. Tradition, in literature, remains of considerable importance. To work with an awareness of tradition is desirable if not necessary if whatever you write is going to have more than an ironic or iconoclastic significance, otherwise the language simply doesn't have enough richness that you can carry that much freight without that kind of awareness. A lot of the power of intensity and ability to change is from an awareness of the layering of the language back through time in this diachronic awareness. I guess the question is "does the language really carry weight and move large areas of meaning of the collective culture and life?"

A Matter of Trust:

Joy Kogawa

The slopes of Christie Pits in west Toronto were covered in snow. As we walked by, two children, one Caucasian and the other Japanese, reached the top of the hill and pulled behind them their bright blue plastic toboggan.

The image stayed with us as we entered Joy Kogawa's house. She showed us into her tidy white living room where we sat on grass mats on the floor. On one wall hung the photograph of a handsome bearded man whom she identified as her grandfather. On a low table beneath the window sat a sandalwood box which looked like an antique camera. She explained that it was a cameraphone, a hand-operated record player which her family had had with them on the long evenings in the evacuation settlement in Slocan, Alberta during World War II. There were other memorabilia about the house that are mentioned in her novel *Obasan*, such as "Yellow Peril", a child's board-game, made in Canada, concerning a war between Japanese and Canadian soldiers. There, as in the novel, on the cover of the box, was the legend repeated in *Obasan*: "The game that shows how a few brave defenders can withstand a very great number of enemies." In the box, there were three blue Canadian pawns and fifty yellow ones. As well, there hung on the wall a fading 1937 Christian Art calendar.

Kogawa, attired in a T'ai Chi' outfit, was amused by our reactions to these artifacts. A sense of great calm and composure filled the house as we followed her from room to room. Finally, she led us back to the front room where she relaxed on a futon bed as she answered our questions.

Joy Kogawa was born in Vancouver in 1935 and, although she was a Canadian citizen, was interned with her family and other Japanese-Canadians during World War II. She has since lived in Saskatoon, Ottawa (where she worked for Prime Minister Trudeau's office and as a Writer-in-Residence at the University of Ottawa) and now resides in Toronto. Her books include the volumes of poetry *The Splintered Moon* (1968), *A Choice of Dreams* (1974), *Jericho Road* (1978), and the children's books *Women In the Woods* (1985), and *Naomi's Robe* (1986). Her novel, *Obasan* (1981) which deals with the wartime evacuation of Japanese-Canadians from the coast of British Columbia, was selected by the Literary Guild Book Club and the Book the the Month Club.

Interviewers: Each of your works, both in poetry and prose, seems to be built around a central thread, a central idea?

Kogawa: Well, there's something that remains with me from each book — a line or two. In *A Splintered Moon* I guess the question I asked is: "What is it in there that says anything?" I think the statement that jumps out at me in there is: "I trust the splintered moon." What I'm saying, basically, is that the kinds of inexact perceptions we have available to us are all that we have to see by. And, however dim it is it is still a kind of seeing that I trust. In each of the books there is a line that says something, that stays with me. In *A Choice of Dreams*, the line is in the poem, "Dear Euclid": "There are patterns more hidden than our patterning / Deaths more lasting than our murdering." And in *Jericho Road* what matters to me most is in the line: "Your surrounding is released by my surrendering." In *Obasan*, the statement is: "Perhaps because I am no longer a child I can know your presence though you are not here." Funnily enough, there seems to be a line in each of my books that matters to me more than any of my other lines.

Interviewers: Why is this so?

Kogawa: Those lines embody insights that I experienced and continue to live by. Each has to do with a fundamental trust, in the face of our limitations, our folly, our abandoning or our abandonment. Everything else dances around these lines.

Interviewers: In A Splintered Moon *your voice is highly introspective yet in your next book,* A Choice of Dreams, *you are the wide-eyed traveller taking everything in...*

Kogawa: In Japan, which I wrote about in the section "About Japan" in *A Choice of Dreams*, I was there as a tourist. I was supposed to be writing poems so I dutifully wrote these poems and took in these perceptions. It was very odd to me that people should have applauded those poems more than those that mattered most to me — the poems about the internal quest. I think it is part of our time that many people view the inward search as a kind of self-indulgence that is not socially relevant, not related sufficiently to the active world. It's judged that the internal world is not the world that binds us. The views today sound more like St. James than St. Paul.

Interviewers: But nonetheless, the internal quest is fulfilling for you personally...

Kogawa: I feel the internal search does reach people. My notion of the Japan poems is that they are like a travelogue.

Interviewers: There is an aura of dislocation and disorientation in the poems about Japan.

Kogawa: I think I carried my dislocation with me to Japan and probably would carry it with me wherever I go. If I had been more fair to what awaited me in Japan, it ought to have been more a sense of coming home because the people were very kind, because there was a sense of my childhood in all the gestures and language habits. Yet, instead of coming home to that, I carried my dislocation with me. Canada is home and I feel dislocated here.

Interviewers: There's a very real sense of dislocation in the poem "Insomnia in a Ryokan."

Kogawa: That poem was about not being able to sleep and not having the same fairy tales as the other people sleeping there, i.e., the mythology is different and I can't, therefore, go out in my neurotic way with my particularly western stories of Cinderella and so on, and demand Prince Charming from my neighbour — that would be incomprehensible to the snoring man next door. In Canada, I can be as neurotic as I am and I'm at home in it. I'm understood. It is accepted that the romantic stories that we grow up with are common to us all. But you have a different mythology in Japan. One thing that struck me when I got on the plane to come home from Japan was that people were talking Freudian stuff. I hadn't heard anything about Oedipal anything over there. Maybe that's because I speak such poor Japanese but I think really you don't hear that kind of psycho-analytical talk there in general.

Interviewers: There are other differences which you've talked about, such as the care of the aged in Japan as compared to here.

Kogawa: This is where I think Hitler won the War. He wanted to present as the ideal society one which was externally beautiful, but which did not care for the feeble and the infirm. Our version of this today can be seen in the overwhelming emphasis which we place on the external beauty of youth. How we can return to caring is something that concerns me. The kind of stories that my mother told me over and over as a child filled me with a sense of tenderness for the old. If our three- or four-year-olds today knew those stories they'd grow up with a sense of: "Oh, aren't those old people dear." That was a part of old Japan. I wonder if young parents in Japan now sit down night after night and tell their children these stories. Maybe that's lost. But I think we can return to that kind of parent-child bonding. I think all kinds of human bonding are good. Here in the West, the emphasis is on the man-woman bonding, which is part of our upbringing — from Adam and Eve and

Cinderella and so on. What about the other bondings, generationally, between parents and children, children and grandparents, siblings, friends, tribes, strangers? Relationships infuse us with a kind of energy. Love does this. It gives us a reason for being. Are we losing that? What kind of mythology do our three and four year-olds derive from the repetition of Coca-Cola ads?

Interviewers: It seems that in the poems about Japan you stress the fact that the Japanese interact as a group — as a community rather than as individuals.

Kogawa: Yes, for instance in the poem about the public baths. I felt a tremendous sense of community in Japan even among strangers. Where that comes from, I'm not sure. There is certainly in Japan a tradition of hospitality especially toward visitors. It's quite excessive. If you are a stranger in Japan they just descend on you with all this attention. But out of that one comes away with a sense of that essential human bonding that matters more than anything else. It is in the structure of the Japanese language that what matters most is the emotional connection between people. What you've got in Japan is a society that for centuries has put a primacy on the emotional interaction between people. It is a highly technological society with robotisation and miniaturisation. But the people are not that way. The people are extremely human in their caring, but not necessarily logical or rationally consistent. Emotions are not particularly reasonable and so irrational thinking is understood, but irrational behaviour is not accepted. In the West, you have the opposite situation, a highly technical language, a technologically-geared language, and, therefore, the minds are roboticised. We tolerate irrational and bizarre individualistic behaviour somewhat better in the West, but we are rational thinkers by and large. What you have are these two cultures with opposing psyches and opposing ways of being and there's a great deal of anxiety when we look at each other and judge each other's behaviour. We'd relax more if we looked less at how we seemed to act and concentrated more on how we think and feel.

Interviewers: Did you have any set image of Japan before you went there?

Kogawa: My image was of this place where trains arrived right on the dime and on the precise second — such rigidity! I found the notions of this terrifying because I was used to so much more freedom. On the other hand, if you were in Japan and looked at the kind of chaos of the structures here in North America you'd be terrified. Here, we strive for community and don't always manage it. We don't have certain foundations that older cultures can take for granted. For instance, we don't have an oral tradition. Various groups have brought their own with them but we have not yet formed our own common one here. There's a vacuum. What demons rush into our empty houses and empty minds? TV? Who stands on guard?

Interviewers: Perhaps they're the artists.

Kogawa: And Canada Council and the CBC, especially Robert Weaver.

Interviewers: You've gone on record as saying that you weren't influenced by any Japanese writers. Have there been others writers that have influenced you?

Kogawa: I don't think I read enough to be influenced by other writers, but the sound of the Japanese language moves me; I don't know how. There's a kind of music, a sound that elicits energy or some strength. But I'm not aware of traditions and forms in literature.

Interviewers: What about the Bible, though? Christian influences and references appear throughout your work.

Kogawa: The Bible matters a lot to me because it was presented in my childhood as this magic thing and I suppose that I still have some Bibliolatry in me and so I use the Bible in this magical way as others use the I Ching or the Tarot. Some of my usage of the Bible is probably at that level of — I suppose it's called — superstition. I respect the Bible as this ancient thing and I attend to it and attend on it. The mythology in it is a pretty strong grid on my mind. I feel it there and I'm not going to chuck it off. I accept that it is this peculiar thing I have learned and have in my background. I accept it for its peculiarity and its uniqueness, but not in any sense for its superiority. The tradition of arrogance within Christianity has been one of the most damaging things that it has had throughout its history. When I think of Christianity or the Bible, it is with almost a sense of shame about the harm that has followed in the history of its arrogance. I think there was a time in Christianity when it was this small fringe movement. It could afford to speak in militant terms because of its weakness. But when it assumed the kind of dominance that it did in society, the militancy was no longer appropriate. That kind of victorious arrogant superiority is still within some churches today, particularly, I think, in fundamentalism. It is horrible and shocking, like pointing to the skeletons in your own closet when you realise that part of the thing you believe in has this awful, awful element to it. What we have to know is that Auschwitz and Hiroshima follow upon two thousand years of Christianity. I don't really discuss these things much within my family which, as you know, is full of clergymen. I don't intend to foist my changes in attitude onto them, or even onto my own kids — but I'm kind of sorry about that sometimes. I guess I'm a closet Christian. But I'm embarrassed about it, especially when I'm among some of my feminist friends who find this aspect of a me a great aberration.

Interviewers: *You've described feminism also as being arrogant, with the woman as victim now often becoming the woman as victimiser...*

Kogawa: I think that's harder to judge because essentially women still are largely marginalised. So, the critique needs to be contained within the context of women's *in camera* examination. But I do see the dangers of arrogance and blindness and jingoism in mass movements which make us lose touch with specifics. We can become so convinced of the reality of our victimisation that we can block from ourselves the full reality of the ways in which we are victimisers — both personally and in groups. If we must not and cannot know about another individual's genuine experience then we are blind to it. That doesn't mean that we shouldn't go out and try to murder a Hitler, but we should always be at least ready to test whether that drive to murder comes from our own individual blind Hitler within.

Interviewers: *In Obasan, the central argument is that it is preferable to become involved in social justice activities only after one has come to know oneself quite thoroughly. If there were to be a sequel to Obasan, and we understand you may be working on one, who would be the more sympathetic character — Aunt Emily, the long-time social-activist, or Naomi, who it would seem by the end of Obasan is prepared, after her journey of self-discovery, to become a social activist on behalf of her people?*

Kogawa: I shouldn't really talk about what I'm working on. It has started and stopped so many times. I certainly do feel that if a person does not withdraw from activism at some time into a kind of contemplation — if we do not question where that activism is leading — if we do not permit doubt, we should at least, realise that we are blind. We can't see around all the corners, but we can at least, perceive with a certain measure of basic trust. We should explore as far as we can our own devious hearts and permit doubt to take us away at some time from our course.

Interviewers: *It seems that in love, doubt, for you, becomes a barrier, an obstacle to the expression of love. For instance, in Obasan, Naomi wants to hug her aunt but cannot, and in various poems of yours there are barriers put up between the lovers because of doubt...*

Kogawa: That's a different kind of doubting. In this instance I think that one ideal is of spontaneity and wholeness, where you feel that rush of passion and you want to go up and throw your arms around someone and trust that the levels of intimacy are appropriate. But in Canada, with its many cultures and messages as to what is appropriate and inappropriate, maybe it explains our reticence. We run up against people who misunderstand and misinterpret gestures of openness and love. One of my problems is that, being brought up to be constrained and restrained it's difficult for me to show emotion openly. But if that style is part of your upbringing, then it is there simply to be accepted, or perhaps to be overcome so that a new freedom can arise and propel one into the next level of intimacy and freedom.

Interviewers: *Dreams also appear to be a propelling mechanism for you both creatively and personally. For instance, you've often spoken about how Obasan was triggered by a dream involving the National Archives of Canada.*

Kogawa: Sometimes dreams are quite overpowering in their insistence and they just break through into the day. They are so strong, and sometimes trumpet their message and meaning. You awaken and the dreams are clearly there, not ephemeral. They have loud messages, with loud insights. Other times my dreams recede and I run after them because I want to know what they are saying. Sometimes, I impose meanings on them. But dreams, for me, became the avenue for finding out what was deeper than my idealism at a time when I knew of no other way. I had gone to the limits of my understanding and my striving, and I was trying to do what seemed to me to be the obvious and right thing in my life. But I simply didn't have the wherewithal to live the life that I believed in. I felt that there might be some avenue of release and direction by way of the not-yet-conscious realm, through the avenue of the dream world. That exploration began in 1964. Dreams, to me, have been very very important. I have gained certain notions from them that stick with me beyond my intellectual quests, that stick with me almost as convictions.

Interviewers: Many of your poems seem to be set in dream-like landscapes where the connections between ideas and images are purely unconscious.

Kogawa: I know some people judge that as a form of conceit. There is such a trust in the concrete world and in concrete imagery and the felt, known, common experiences of us all, that it's judged to be a kind of dishonesty to venture off into this other landscape that is not so commonly concrete and known. I believe these worlds of experience are connected and we need dialogue among our different views. In regard to pro-lifers, part of me honours the fact that they are willing to enter that metaphysical world of the fetus' consciousness. However, if I had to choose between a metaphysical reality that I would put on the level of principles and ideals and the actual concrete, felt reality of human suffering I would have to choose for this world's reality — which is why I would at this stage of my understanding about suffering be a pro-choice person. Both pro-choice and pro-life activists are anti-suffering. I would say that the reality of people who are alive now and who are conscious now and who are suffering is somehow demanding of my response more than the principle of potential consciousness within human cells. Plants, for instance, seem to show sign of sentient life. I understand they recoil at being cut. I believe that sentient life is all around us, but we have an immediate

responsibility to conscious suffering. I think principles are not just hypothetical things, and I cling very much to that other world of principles and dreams and the "consciousness" within cells and plants — all of that is very real to me. Nevertheless, given the choice between being responsible for that and being responsible to a fellow human being who is suffering, I will respond to that fellow human being. Arrogantly imposing a metaphysic on others is what Christianity has been guilty of throughout its history. Hans Küng says: "Christianity is the most murderous religion there has ever been." Christians have still to learn humility and will no doubt have to face humbling.

Interviewers: What about a poem, like "Dear Euclid" where you appear to be more concerned about prenatal life?

Kogawa: There's no doubt about that concern or about a tenderness toward the unborn child. There's also no doubt about unendurable realities involved in the choice to abort. But, in the last lines of "Dear Euclid", the dead moon says it is indestructible. Therefore, if the dream can be trusted, you don't have to go around desperately campaigning for that life because it is not destroyed. At least, that is what the moon says. In the meantime, we've got real human suffering here and we have to attend to it. Our energy belongs here. I think it is possible, of course, for all of us to be right or wrong in this matter and I think we need more dialogue, but right now the air feels full of rage.

Interviewers: In relation to rage, you've been very involved in lobbying Ottawa for both an apology about what happened to Japanese-Canadians during World War II and also for reparations for their material losses during that period. But you've encountered a lot of opposition, not only from Federal politicians and bureaucrats, but also from many members of the Japanese-

Canadian community. *What do you feel about that opposition, especially that from Japanese-Canadians?*

Kogawa: Agony! I feel sick about the whole thing. What I've discovered is that I am extremely limited in my capacity for political involvement. Some people don't mind being verbally attacked or misinterpreted. Some people seem to be able to stride through that kind of thing. I can't do that. I'm just overcome by it. In fact, this year, from time to time, I've wanted to leave Canada, especially Toronto, because I couldn't stand it. During those few months I was in Japan, I heard Trudeau's remarks about an apology not being warranted, and I didn't really want to come back. But on the other hand, where else is there to be? This is my home. I'd like to close my ears to it all but then the phone rings, and I get calls from people in the community. You have no idea how much hurting there is in this whole thing. The generational schism created for political motives is shocking. So I've felt that what I need to do is say nothing at all and I've tried to stay out of things unless my arm's being twisted right off.

Interviewers: You once said that your silence about Japanese-Canadians in World War II was tantamount to a betrayal of your people.

Kogawa: Yes, I did feel that, and I felt compelled to speak out, and I discovered that a few people were choosing to tell some of the older generation that my speaking out was disgracing and betraying them. It's a quicksand world of betrayal and expressions of betrayal. Enmity is created by the will to see the enemy. That makes it hard to speak at all, so, there comes another kind of silence. There is the kind of silence that cannot speak and the kind that will not speak. I want to withdraw to the pen.

Interviewers: You've said that the character of Aunt Emily in Obasan is based on Muriel

Kitagawa, a Japanese-Canadian activist like yourself.

Kogawa: She was a young woman in Vancouver, who was married and had children, and who wrote these letters to her brother, Wes, who was a medical student in Toronto and who is now a leader within the National Association of Japanese-Canadians. After the war she ended up staying with James Finlay's family. Finlay was the chairman of the Co-operative Committee on Japanese-Canadians, as is mentioned at the end of *Obasan*. Muriel died quite a number of years ago and I came across her manuscripts and letters. In 1977, as a result of my dream about the Archives, I went to Ottawa. I needed some photographs of Coaldale, Alberta for an article I was writing, and Mark Hopkins, who worked at the Archives, showed me Muriel's letters. I was very moved by them. She became some sort of presence. Her husband, Ed Kitagawa, lives in Toronto. In my first draft of *Obasan* it was Aunt Muriel rather than Aunt Emily, but I felt I should replace the name Muriel with Emily because I had never met Muriel. I didn't know what she looked like, and I didn't want her family to be offended in any way. So I used the name Emily. I'm not sure it was the right name but there it is.

Interviewers: You've posed the question, "How does society stop oppressing those who cannot speak up?" Is this the test of a caring society?

Kogawa: A feminist theologian, Rosemary Ruether, has an answer to that question — a question about a world of peace without victims. She has written an essay in the book, *Anti-Semitism and the Foundations of Christianity*, in which she says: "Each of us must discover the secret key to divine abandonment that God has abandoned divine power into the human condition utterly and completely that we may not abandon one another." What I get from that is that there is no God who is going to come down and rescue us, but that the power we once invested in that belief is now within us to rescue those who are abandoned. That power is real. It is within the human condition. We have the capacity to unleash the power of the atom, and, the capacity to unleash that amazing explosion of compassion, in infinitesimal thoughts and decisions. I do believe this.

Interviewers: So, as in Obasan, *as long as you care you are not abandoned?*

Kogawa: The beginning of Naomi's release from the dead world of unanswered questions is when she begins to become so absorbed in caring for her aunt that she stops asking about her mother. It is at that point that the dream comes forth, the answer to her question comes forth, and it comes with the understanding of what happened to her mother and the beginning of her realisation that she was not abandoned, despite all the evidence, despite all her experience. At the end of the book she holds her head a certain way. She can smell, from where she is, the faint hint, the skin-thin evidence, that there is love there — the evidence is faint as the whiff of a rose. But that is enough. It is a beginning. There's a source of love that breaks through into dreams and is rooted in the underground stream, and what we have to do is recognise the evidence.

Interviewers: Are we to take it that Naomi would have been quite a different person if in 1954 when Aunt Emily came to visit she had at that point found out that her mother had died as a result of the atomic bomb explosion over Nagasaki? Would she have become more of an Aunt Emily character than the character she became?

Kogawa: I had never thought of that. But what I suspect is that we never hear until we are ready to. We only come to the capacity to see when our eyes have been made ready. Whether she had been told or not she might

not have been able to absorb that with the kind of realisation or the kind of love that was possible for her at the time of her caring for her aunt.

Interviewers: The New York Times *said of* Obasan *that for you history was not a "progression of events but a repetition of restlessness."*

Kogawa: Wouldn't Eli Mandel say that? If I were to draw an analogy between my personal history and history in the public sense, I think it is that there are things to learn and that we keep repeating and repeating the lessons until we learn them. Once we learn them, we don't have to repeat them anymore. We go from learning to learning. So, it's important to deal with the past in order for the lesson to be learned. In some areas we're slow learners but I think there are some changes in other areas. What matters most to me is that we should learn some basic fundamental trust. I think we cannot trust until we are trusted, just as we cannot love until we are loved. I think that the precondition of trusting is a willingness to perceive that we are trusted in the midst of evidence that we are not, a willingness to sift out the evidence that shows us the existence of trust. We have faced full-front the reality of evil and now have a crisis of trust in ourselves so that looking for the evidence that we do trust, that we are trusted, is not an easy task. But miners used to go out and sift for gold with their little pans. Well, we're out there today doing that in great numbers. That's what we need now — people who are willing to go out and pan for gold, to pan for trust.

In Search of
The Dead:

In front of our hotel, there was a small dock on the river, and a sign which promised that the next ferry would be along in ten minutes or less. The hands of the clock on the ferry sign were missing and the river was completely frozen over. As we stood on the dock we heard somebody calling out to us. We turned and saw Patrick Lane coming toward us, swathed in a long red scarf, ear muffs, and a heavy beige coat. He said he wanted to get some fresh air before we did the interview, so we walked along the south bank of the Saskatchewan River.

The snow had fallen a few weeks before and the remnants clung in muddy patches in the hard earth. Blackbirds and ravens darted in and out of the dried grey bullrushes that were frozen along the shore. As we walked past a number of residential side-streets, we noticed a poster, protesting the Federal government's Free Trade Proposals, that was left fluttering from a telephone pole in the wake of the November 1988 election. The poster denounced, in no uncertain terms, the Minister of Trade, John Crosbie. Lane stopped to look at the poster and remarked, "We take our politics pretty seriously out here. Kinda looks like a wanted poster, doesn't it?" He turned away from the poster and walked determinedly over towards the front lawn of a United Church where a cardboard crèche had been set up for the Advent season. The problem was that St. Joseph's neck was worn through and limp, and the figure nodded agreeably in the wind. Lane laughed, "as you can see we take our religion pretty seriously, too. Welcome to Saskatoon, guys."

Patrick Lane was born in Nelson, B.C. in 1939, and educated at the University of British Columbia. He has worked in logging, fishing, mining, trucking, retailing, and teaching. With bill bissett and Seymour Mayne, he established the small press Very Stone House in the early Sixties. His poetry collections include *Letters from a Savage Mind* (1966), *Separations* (1969), *Mountain Oysters*

(1972), *The Sun Has Begun to Eat the Mountains* (1972), *Beware the Months of Fire* (1973), *Unborn Things: Poems of South America* (1975), *Albino Pheasants* (1977), *Poems New and Selected* (1979, for which he won the Governor General's Award), *The Measure* (1980), *Old Mother* (1982), *Woman In the Dust* (1983), *Selected Poems* (1987), and *Winter* (1990). He co-wrote with Lorna Crozier *No Longer Two People* (1981). He edited the work of his brother, Red Lane, who died in 1964 — *The Collected Poems of Red Lane* (1968). He lives in Saskatoon with Lorna Crozier. This interview was conducted in Saskatoon, December 8, 1988.

Interviewers: You wrote No Longer Two People *with Lorna Crozier and a question we asked her — and we wanted to get your response to it — how did the book come about?*

Lane: There are two things that happened. We are both writers and we were also in the middle of an affair, which had transformed itself suddenly into us living together with all the energy involved in that because she was still married to someone else and I had a relationship going and also had kids. We were both in the process of breaking up with old relationships and starting this new relationship and neither of us was very sure about all of this. At the same time we were also competing and confronting each other very strongly. I just vaguely remember Lorna and I drinking one night and getting into one of our usual arguments, which only lovers can really get into, one of those passionate arguments which almost always end up with you going to bed together, one of the mechanisms for getting to bed and then you solve all of the world's problems. I think I went to bed because I couldn't take the argument anymore. I did the typical male thing which was to say "why don't we go to bed, sleep, get up in the morning and discuss it." And the woman always says "let's argue it out to the end now." There's

always this confrontation between the male idea of postponement and the female idea of immediate solution. I went to bed. Lorna was sitting there very angry at me and she wrote this poem, walked in and threw it at me. She said "there, that's for you." I got up and looked at this poem and thought I just can't leave it at that, so I got up and wrote a poem in answer to it and suddenly we began communicating through our typewriters rather than actually arguing. That night, I think, we wrote about four poems, which are the first four poems in the book. And then we thought, as only writers can, what an interesting idea. It was actually Lorna's idea to continue, not mine. My idea was to leave it there — I didn't want to continue. She said, let's push it, let's see what happens.

Interviewers: You seem to be reaching a kind of intense energy in your relationship with Lorna Crozier. Do women provide you with the energy to write?

Lane: I've always needed the female principle with me as a nurturing source of energy, with which I interact all the time. The five years that I was on my own between my first marriage and my second marriage drove me crazy. My first wife was a better poet than I was when I first started out. She never pursued it. She was writing much better poems than I was in the early Sixties. I went and published her poems in *Blew Ointment*, a magazine bill bisset produced and she was very upset and never wrote again. But she was a better poet than I was.

Interviewers: Were you surprised by the hostile reaction to No Longer Two People?

Lane: There was a tremendous amount of hostility to the book, a lot of which I didn't understand. Many people were angry at us because they felt it was a book of confessional poetry, and it wasn't confessional poetry. It didn't work from any of the confessional realism that you find in Anne Sexton or any of the great New England confessional schools of autobiographical reality, given that we were working out our own feelings and our own experiences. We were exploring the mythological world, a world that existed on a variety of other planes. Other poets have begun exploring the same thing — Terry Heath and Anne Szumigalski have done dialogues.

Interviewers: It was almost like Leonard Cohen's Death of a Lady's Man where you have the male and female halves of the brain arguing with each other — but the critics didn't like that very much, either.

Lane: Few people have read Cohen properly in the last ten years. No one approaches what he has tried to do at all. I don't know whether it is the world of criticism or the desire of the reading public, (which is a critical public after all) but there is a desire on their part for a writer to remain in a place where he or she can be understood. They get very upset when a writer goes through a process of change. Change is a part of the endurance of being a writer. If you endure the process long enough eventually something will occur, and then you suddenly move onto another plateau. You suddenly say, "oh, now I'm here." It is suddenly a very different place than where you had been before. There are those writers who refuse change because they are afraid of what that might do.

Interviewers: You said once that you were trying to break away from what you considered to be "the Patrick Lane poem."

Lane: Yeah.

Interviewers: Do you feel that the poems you are writing now are more meditative?

Lane: Strangely enough, I come around to the poems at the end of my *Selected Poems* (1987) and I find that those poems are still Pat Lane poems although they are more meditative, or more elegiac perhaps. I've gone back, in a sense, to very early narrative forms and structures so I really haven't escaped many of the forms that I earlier explored.

Interviewers: The more recent works seem to meditate on philosophical concerns rather than trying to startle by turning images upside down. The earlier poems seemed to be hallmarked by the startling image whereas the more recent ones make their claims by being more sombre and controlled and subdued reflections, such as a poem like "Night."

Lane: Although there *are* very startling images in "Night." I guess what you mean is that the earlier poems had more violence about them?

Interviewers: Yes.

Lane: A rooster with its beak cut off. There's a startling quality to the image which shocks.

Interviewers: You can hear a bit of A. Alvarez "Against the Gentility Principle" in the background.

Lane: I'd never thought of that. That's interesting. I feel more sombre now. I'm not twenty-five years old any more. I'm fifty years old. My perceptions, the way I view the world has changed. The way I think has changed a great deal. Moving to the Prairie I've found a home here — home in the sense of not the original fantasy home with Mom and Dad, the place we all try to escape from, and the recognition that that home probably never did exist, but suddenly deciding to find a place, a locus, a nexus that you can operate out of, which for me became the Prairie. Why I've chosen the Prairie, I don't know, other than I think of it as a forgotten place in a forgotten time. It doesn't exist in the larger political, economic, socio-cultural world, so consequently you can drop into this world and drop out of the other world.

Interviewers: Often, when Prairie writers approach that landscape as a mental construct, they deal with it as a place that is out of place, which is Eli Mandel's view of it. In one of his photographs he has a door in the middle of the Prairie which leads from nowhere to nowhere.

Lane: That's very much Mandel's generation, and Kroetsch's generation as well. They were the first generation who had to suffer deeply the process of becoming an immigrant within their own country. They were the first generation to become aware of having left a place and not being able to regain it. I don't think earlier writers felt that at all. You go back to the Confederation poets, or even as recently as Frank Scott, and you still have people who have a solid sense of where home is. I think that writers like Mandel suddenly felt themselves displaced. For my generation, to be displaced was to be home. But for them, they were caught in this interface between the ideal home and the idea that where they were was no home at all.

   They couldn't regain the original and where they were was not a gainable place. For our generation, to be displaced is to be permanently at home anywhere. For them it was to be at home nowhere. Kroetsch's endless desire to recapture some image of the Prairie, some original place, means a desire to place the Prairie in some sort of ordered vision of the world. Mandel's return, to search through the graveyard for some sort of original spot where he could identify himself, and then finding that all there was was a graveyard, culminates in that shattering moment when he meets someone on the street who remembers his father. I seldom go back to the town where I grew up in and try to find someone who remembers my father or who remembers me.

It never occurs to me. I live in a world of permanent displacement. I am a twentieth century man.

Interviewers: Are you saying you don't have a home?

Lane: It is not a home that is locked into geographical time and place.

Interviewers: You define the home yourself rather than being defined by it.

Lane: Yes. Very much so.

Interviewers: Weren't writers like Mandel and Kroetsch, though, responding to the larger literary themes of twentieth century alienation and isolation? Mandel talks a lot about Kafka, picks up images from films such as The Marathon Man, for instance — that whole sense of someone who is constantly on the move.

Lane: That's very true. These were men, and women — I can think of Miriam Waddington who struggles in her poems with issues from the Thirties, like Sacco and Vanzetti, and the great movements of the Twenties and the Thirties, and her parents who were immigrants and their vision of the world that was tied into Europe and grand traditions of revolutions, etc. In her poems she talks about being a middle-aged professor living in the suburbs of Toronto and she has no locus, no place anywhere, but there's a dream place somewhere back in time where everything was real and everything had value. It was tied in very much to the prewar world and the war itself.

Interviewers: It seems like Mandel is living in the vacuum of that disappearance but he still has a central-European imagination.

Lane: Mandel, as well as Layton, suffer from a certain angst which is tied into not only the east-European tradition but also into the

Jewish image of the holocaust — the guilt because they lived. They have to live with the fact that they survived at all. But to go on with the idea of home. I don't see home as the Okanagan Valley. Last year I was invited to go back and read in Nelson, the town I was born in. My mother and father lived in a little mining town way off in the mountains, a little place called Sheepcreek. About twenty years ago I went back up there with my mother, after my father was murdered, mostly as a form of a healing experience for my mother. She had developed cancer because of the emotional shock of having lost her husband. I took her on this journey back in time thinking that if I took her back there she would grow back into this world and find herself again. And she went with me back to this place called Sheepcreek which doesn't exist anymore. It's a classic Canadian town.

Interviewers: Like Al Purdy's Wooller, Ontario.

Lane: It's particularly like that in the West. After the miners moved out they moved the whole town. Nothing was left. It is the same on the Prairies here. Once the grain elevators go, the whole town is packed up and moved. Even the graveyards are erased. Nothing is left. There is no record. Europe doesn't know this. In Europe all the villages still exist. They are permanent records of man's inhabitancy. In the western part of North America, there is no permanent record. This record is constantly being obliterated and new records are being created and there is no history.

Interviewers: So what happened in Sheepcreek?

Lane: The first time I went back, my mother had trouble finding the place. The trees had grown up over the twenty years she'd been gone. The next time I went back in 1988, the spruce were about forty-five years old, but I managed to find where we lived. All that was left was the clothes line stand my mother had

stood on when I first took her there. Then I went to the back of the house where people had thrown their garbage. So, I'm digging down through layers of moss and dirt, etc. and finding tin cans and bottles. As I dig down through the detritus of their lives when they lived there for ten years, I find the Pacific Milk cans from the milk I drank when I was a little boy. So, I'm searching through my own past and finally I get down to the point where there is no more refuse, but just dirt — pre-history. It was one of the most amazing sort of things. I walked out of there thinking, "what was I searching for? What made me dig down through all those layers of dirt like some sort of insane sentimental archeologist, searching for what?"

Interviewers: But in a strange way, this is what Purdy is searching for in his poems of Ameliasburgh, as are a lot of other Canadian writers. We've been displaced, not only geographically from home, but from time, and we're trying to recreate our own past.

Lane: I choose to live in Saskatoon because there I find a world which imitates the idealised world I came out of, though it is not the same.

Interviewers: One of the concepts that seems to be an undercurrent in Canadian literature is that you don't really exist until you invent yourself, and in order to do that you have to find a place of your own, and find out just how far time goes in that spot. You seem to be doing that in your poem "The Weight."

Lane: Yes. I wrote "The Weight" because of Andrew Suknaski's "Wood Mountain Poems." I could identify with Sukaski's western search more than Purdy's eastern search. I never felt the identity with all of Purdy's preoccupations with the old mill and Owen Roblin. He could talk about a three hundred year history in Ontario. For me, I couldn't identify with that. Where I grew up we didn't have a history of longer than a hundred years. When Andy Suknaski began writing about Wood Mountain — and that book came out in the early Seventies — I was struck by his search back through his past. Also Barry Mackinnon's poems as well — his search for some kind of historical relationship. Basically, all I was trying to say in "The Weight" was that as soon as you begin to search back into that kind of a time and there is no one from that time to tell you about it — essentially what the Indians think of as time, is an ongoing three-generation flux so that the only witness you have is a father and grandfather and prior to that no one existed and time didn't exist — so that the only known world is the oral world, a world that can be reported directly. If things cannot be reported directly they do not exist. They become spiritual, mythological, and in a sense aesthetic. I was suddenly struck with the fact that I wanted to record where I had come from because I had read Suknaski's poem. I suddenly realised that I had no witnesses. I had no father, no grandfather. I had no one to give me the record. Therefore, I had to invent that from remembered stories. At that point I was involved in the meaning of fiction, which is "the lie." I was inventing the world, at which point I rejected that at the end, because that becomes history and history too becomes a lie. I was very confused in terms of who I felt I was as a man. I remembered my father being a rodeo rider. I was told these things. These were real things. But I thought, they weren't real things. They were told to me when I was a little boy and I fantasised them. He became 'the MacLeod kid.' Did he really exist? Because I can't go back and ask my father whether he was lying to me when he told me that story. Was he really a rodeo rider? Did I invent that story? Then I became lost in the flux of my own personal history, asking myself did anything really happen to me?

Interviewers: Is that what you mean by what you said in 1979 to Poetry Canada Review *where you stated you don't really believe your poetry is classically autobiographical, and that there's a danger in reading it as such?*

Lane: That's true. I have a great deal of difficulty reading my very early poems in performance now. I get very confused by the persona in the poems because I don't even remember who that person was twenty years ago. I can go back to early poems like "Carnival Man" and I can't, in my mind's eye, create the visual image of myself sitting in a room writing that poem. When I read that poem I'm no longer that person, and I don't know who that guy was. I have no idea who that person was. I don't remember.

Interviewers: So, history, then, is a matter of perspective rather than record.

Lane: Yes. History is what somebody else tells you. It is your faith that he is telling you the truth. I trust that my father's story was as real to him as his grandfather's story was to him. But whether any of if happened, I don't know. As a writer I invent things constantly. I'm willing to change reality for the sake of language, for the sake of the poem. I'm willing to do anything to reality to make it a greater reality.

Interviewers: Is that behind a line, for instance, like "we've been together so long now none of us can remember when we began to be each other," (from "The Silence Game") that flow of lives into each other.

Lane: Yes. I think so. And we play the silence game. Most poets I know play with silence all the time. It is one of their preoccupations, one of their obsessions, one of their idiosyncrasies. They delight in silence. The making of a poem is the making of silence, in an odd way. To create an utterance is to create a great silence because you aren't speaking any more. You can stay outside of that forever. When

I'm alone in my dialogue, with whoever that happens to be — you can call him the mythical reader — I am talking into a profound silence when I'm at my typewriter or when I'm at the pen or the computer. One of the things that poetry does is that it resists analysis, it resists interpretation, it resists understanding. The really great poems are the ones you go back to again and again and again, trying to understand, and if they continue to resist they become truly great; in a sense they become a reflection of silence.

Interviewers: So, silence itself is a form of resistance.

Lane: Yes.

Interviewers: What kind of silence exists in your poems, then, because there are all kinds of silence: the Japanese concept of silence as something present and alive in its own right as David Wevill suggested; there's Robert Bly's silence which is almost Bly's voice breaking the silence; or the English poetic sense of silence as an absence...

Lane: When you confront a loved poem, and each person has their "loved poem" if they care at all about language, you sit with this enigmatic object in front of yourself, you sing to yourself and read it out loud, you read it to yourself silently, and you are left with this profoundly important object which is completely silent. It only lives when you make it live.

Interviewers: But there is the paradox of something in the poem called "the voice."

Lane: Which is what the poet strives for.

Interviewers: What British poet, Christopher Middleton, calls "the endophone," that sense of the poet within the poem which cannot be displaced through time — he says you can still hear Keats' accent in one of his poems.

Lane: And hopefully you can still hear my accent in my poems. Talk to any of my peers — Newlove, Atwood, and the accent of their poems is not necessarily the accent of their lives. The voice you find in poems is not necessarily your *"normal"* voice. You adopt a mask, you create a persona, and that is a very strange, magical moment.

Interviewers: There's a five year hiatus in your biography from the Sixties when you did a lot of travelling. Do you think that travelling helped you?

Lane: Travelling is important for Canadians. It is very different than the European idea of travelling. When a European travels, especially in the nineteenth century idea of travel, he goes to broaden his horizons by experiencing mutually identical cultures. When a Canadian travels it is to find a place, again, to find home, because there is no place in Canada where you can say *you are.* Home exists in language. So, for the writer, language is the essential home, the place where you locate yourself. I know all kinds of Canadian writers and most of them are well-read, historically astute, remarkable people from Milton Acorn through Al Purdy, from Margaret Avison through to Miriam Waddington. They know more about the historical world than writers I've met from other countries. The historical world doesn't exist here, physically. Canadians travel in order to find a historical world. They go elsewhere to say, "ah, yes, the human species has existed somewhere for some length of time." When they come back to Canada it is such a completely transient world. We don't have history here, particularly in the West. For us it is to flee a place that hasn't yet been named and go to the assurance of a place that has been named. It is wonderful, for a Canadian, to go for the first time to London or Paris or Moscow or New Delhi or Cusco, to go to a place on which they can't impose themselves. To go outward from Canada is to lose yourself in an historical world. When I first saw Cusco in South America in 1972, I was struck by the fact that something old existed in a sophisticated way. I could come to Canada and find petroglyphs, scratchings upon stone, the most ephemeral of records that indicated that man had been here before. But to go to Central and South America and wander there, as I did for a couple of years in the early Seventies, is to find the record of profoundly edifying civilisations that had existed and passed away. As a Canadian, this was incredible because I had no knowledge of this in my own northern civilisation. One of the things that North America loves about itself is that it is a history-less place. They celebrate that constantly. They are the *avant garde* of place and time because they come from a place without history.

Interviewers: It is interesting that Québecois have a different sense of time, as something stretching out both behind them and in front of them.

Lane: That's because they are a lost people.

Interviewers: Yes. Québecois literature keeps stressing that they are lost in a wilderness of time.

Lane: Precisely. It is the same as the Scots/ Irish of the Maritimes — they are lost in time. They are secure in that they know there was a time when they existed, and they transplanted the whole time over here, which is what Alistair MacLeod says. They transplanted that time over here at which point time ceased to exist. I remember being at a conference in Cape Breton where a bunch of Scots poets and scholars came over here to go and talk to people in old-age homes to get the original dialect, the old Gaelic language. They came here to find *their* history because they knew that their history had been entombed in Canada. History stopped moving once they

got here. That's really, really important to the Canadian character because we are a constant tomb for history.

Interviewers: On the topic of South America, you dedicated the Macchu Picchu poem, originally, to both Earle Birney and Pablo Neruda, and then you very quietly dropped Neruda from the dedication on the reprint version of the poem. Why?

Lane: That's a really interesting question. I went to South America for a variety of reasons, one of which was Neruda.

Interviewers: Did you ever meet Neruda?

Lane: I never got to Chile, which was why, about a year ago I went to Chile as a way of correcting, not so much a failing of nerve, but of ideal, perhaps. I went down to South America originally with the idea of meeting Neruda. I'd been reading him, and at that time no one else went to South America. I was really trying to lose myself there. I wanted to disappear out of time and place. I wanted to go away from home and I didn't want to go to Europe or Asia or the places everyone else was going in the late Sixties and early Seventies. What I discovered was that I'd gone precisely to the place that resembled my home the most. I went to the west coast of South America, and its geography was precisely the same as the place I'd grown up in our Rocky Mountains. I found myself almost right back home again and that disturbed the hell out of me (Laughter). I thought, Christ, I've gone to a place where I won't exist and here I am existing more than I can imagine. My first knowledge of Macchu Picchu came from reading Neruda and also reading Neruda's political poems. I was never a political writer in the overt rhetorical sense. I never believed the way Tom Wayman believes, that you can take poetry and get the masses repeating your poems and raging away, and suddenly they all go out in the streets and kill the soldiers, and everything is a beautiful world after that. I never believed that. I grew up in the working class and the working class doesn't think that way. Anyway, when I went to South America, I refused to go to Chile because Chile was a hassle for me. It was right at the moment of Allende and all the problems there. I'd already gone through a revolution in Columbia and all kinds of hassles in Ecuador and Peru and I thought, I'm not going to go into the middle of a revolution. I don't need this in my life. For me, the last thing I want to be a part of is a bunch of people shooting each other with submachine guns. So, I backed away from it. The reason I dropped Neruda on the later printing of the poem was because I became disillusioned with Neruda. When I finally read through the Neruda poems I suddenly thought, it's all very well for an upper class individual to feel the deep and profound need of the lower classes, to raise them up. I suddenly saw Neruda for what he really was — the son of a wealthy family, whose uncles and aunts were senators, who came from the most privileged classes of Chile. Neruda was put up with by the powers that be in his day until finally he escaped over the mountains, assisted by a couple of peasants who helped him through the passes and trails. It is one of the great mythic stories of Chile, of Neruda travelling over the mountains to escape to Argentina, forgetting the fact that, and this is the part of the story I love, that Neruda rode the donkey all the way and the two peasants walked. I love that part of the story. It permanently, exquisitely, delineates the upper class. I can see Neruda riding on the donkey writing his great diatribes against the powers that be while the two ordinary poor workers are guiding him over the mountain. Without them he'd have died in ten minutes in the mountains. The reason I pulled Neruda's name off the poem was because I thought to myself, I'm up to here with the upper class desire for the change for the masses. The

masses never change. If I've known one thing in the fifty years I've lived it's that the masses never change. The masses are in permanent and perpetual misery out of which they find exquisite moments of happiness. Some of the great moments of happiness I've known in my life have been moments with ordinary people, working people, out of whom I come. Those moments are great fun. You drink, you laugh, you dance, forget tomorrow, to hell with it. Your unemployment insurance is going to get cut off tomorrow? Good, let's go get drunk tonight. It is a moment of celebration. The upper classes cannot imagine doing this. They can't imagine a moment where people sit together in a kitchen and say "tomorrow is the last day of unemployment insurance and after that we face nothing." At that point the working classes say let's go to the bar, get drunk and dance. The upper classes say "how dare they do that. Don't they care? Don't they worry about this? Do they see how important it is?" And the working classes say, "Worry? What's worry? I've been worried since I was born and the fact of the matter is, at this point, this moment of impasse, all you can do is dance. What else is there to do?"

Interviewers: So, you're saying the working class has no sense of time?

Lane: They have no sense of time. Time is always a virtue imposed from above. The masses don't exist in history. Time is imposed by the upper classes, never the lower classes.

Interviewers: But isn't time a form of a trap? If you have a past, aren't you tapped by it as well as defined by it? You wrote the essay "To the Outlaw." Do you still believe what you said in that back in the early Seventies?

Lane: I believe what the essay says. I'm a little embarrassed by the Rimbaudian voice of the essay. I wish I could rewrite it. But I still stand behind those words all the way. Where I say to hell with these guys who are teaching in the universities, although I'm now temporarily teaching in the university and I'm happy to get the money. It is nice to finally make a living for a while. So I would temper things that way. At the same time I would joyfully join the vision of the young man to the older man. The young man is still the older man.

Interviewers: You've professed, on several occasions, that you have a preoccupation with technique.

Lane: I saw Andy Suknaski last week and he said "Lane, you're very different from me." And I said, "yeah, I know." And he said "my poems are made out of water. You sculpt your poems out of rock. I read your poems and they are carved."

Interviewers: There's something definite about the images.

Lane: "They're absolute," he said. "They're carved in stone. They're just there. You can't move your poems. My poems you can move anywhere. They shift and change all the time." And I agree. Why, I don't know. Both Suknaski and I are fascinated by form and structure, yet the poetry is very different.

Interviewers: Your South American poems are very formally structured.

Lane: That was the first time that I admitted to myself that I knew anything about the formal, historical values of literature. I said, I know all these things, why don't I just write them in these terms, and play with these structures. I built poems, not out of imitations of what other people had done, but I allowed what I knew to extend itself into my writing, which was the moment I became a writer, really. Before that I hadn't really done the important work of my life. So, what is this new classicism? A movement away from the vernacular voice, a movement away from the nineteenth century idea, the Keatsian, the Shellian, the great romantic idea that somewhere out there is a great unwashed individual writer who will suddenly leap out in Rimbaud-like fashion and make a great rhetoric out of his own speech. I suddenly knew that nowhere ever has this occurred in history. Even the Rimbaud that we know was deeply schooled in the grand tradition of his language. What he did was he paraphrased and recreated, out of the tradition, the echo of the modern, because the modern is never there, you can never hold on to it. All a great writer does is create out of the great tradition, all the memories and echoes of the tradition, with the edge of the new. The edge of the new is always within the identities you find in the content. I remember in the early Seventies experimenting with blank verse, largely because I thought this is where I will find it. I remember reading William Carlos Williams and discovering that much of what he wrote was buried iambic pentameter. In spite of his attempt to make it new, in spite of his attempt to make a new American voice, he was perhaps more conservative in his approach to verse than Pound was, who hated it. Pound was far more experimental than Williams. I suddenly saw this. I suddenly saw Williams breaking the poem up on the page to hide the fact that he was, in a sense, working out of the great tradition. I went back and read all of the great poets again — Dante and whoever — and I saw them echoing, profoundly, this great traditional process.

Interviewers: But you had to go outside Canadian literature for that.

Lane: Of course. Because at the time I thought nothing in Canadian literature coincided.

Interviewers: But you can feel a rhythm, sometimes, in your verse of Pound and Eliot. Are you conscious of doing that or is that a product of your reading?

Lane: It is funny now, as I get older, and I read people like Atwood, Newlove or others from our generation from around the world and suddenly, because I'm getting older and remember more and more, I see the echoes of other people appearing all the time in their verse. I suddenly realise where Newlove came out of Rilke, for example. He'd been reading Rilke since he was nineteen. I see where Phyllis Webb came out of this person or that person and I say, "Isn't that wonderful." What happens is that you marry rhythms and patterns in your own mind. You marry them exquisitely and passionately. You love them. Then ten years down the road you pull those wonderful rhythms and patterns out of your mind and you remake them. That's what's called "the tradition." It's called being in love with death.

Interviewers: Explain.

Lane: Because all patterns and rhythms that come from outside of yourself are the utterances of those who are dead. Even when I read, as a young man in Vernon, British Columbia, Wallace Stevens, T.S. Eliot, Pound were all alive. But they were all dead men to me. When I read my first confessional poetry of Anne Sexton, she was dead to me because she didn't exist. She wasn't there. All I had was her language, and her language was no different than Thucydides or whoever. To me, all language, as it existed on the page, was the language of the dead who were kept alive by the language. I grew up as a child with the idea that everyone was dead. For me, in Vernon, in the library which was in the fire hall, which was made up of books left over from English immigrants, old leather bound volumes of Hardy and Dickens, of all the books I read when I was a kid everyone who wrote was dead. One of the most disturbing

things in my life was actually to discover that there were living writers, and I didn't discover that until I was almost twenty-three.

Interviewers: Why did you have that notion that the book was a finality, that it was almost a tombstone?

Lane: It came from reading those books in that firehall. They were old and musty. Tombstones are, on one level, the record of the mouldering dead, but they are also an affirmative gesture of the dead to the living. To me, that was profoundly important.

Interviewers: Isn't that because, at least here in Canada, we're always the last ones to hear about things? Take for instance the fact that you couldn't walk into the bookstores of Toronto and find contemporary British and American poetry until very recently. You had to go to England to find out what was being written there, and in our language.

Lane: But even having gone there, be honest, having gone there and coming back here, and having gone to the right bookstores in Toronto and you get the right books, you can never catch up. You never are on top of the world. To be a Canadian is not to be on top of the world. Say you two guys moved to New York, and instead of interviewing Patrick Lane you interview whoever is there, and every time you interview somebody it is never quite the interview it should be because the ultimate interview is the great living interview. You guys sit and you do tombstone reality because you measure things. This is a measured world that you are creating here. Out of this rambling conversation we're having here, we're really searching among the tombstones of the dead. We're wandering in search of what? We wander in search of the dead. We do not search for the living. Canadians do not do it, number one. Americans aren't good at searching for the dead, but we are. All of our novels and our poems are concerned with it. I love that about Canadian literature — the necrophilia — because that's who we are and we're good at it. You're good at it. Somebody has to look after graveyards. Oddly enough, I've always thought of our being behind the times as a privilege, because we're the last people to hear about it, aren't we lucky? Between the moment of somebody making or doing something and us hearing about it, we have a hiatus where we're allowed to do something on our own. There are some who would argue for a nineteenth century idea of what Canada is and that is really not important. What they're really talking about is time to reflect and time to play. One of the lovely things about being a satellite, not a colony because we've stopped being a colony, is to always be able to reflect, like the moon. You can look down at the bigger planet and say, "isn't that interesting," and mull it over for a while. I love that about Canada. I remember sitting in Vernon once, years ago, and saying "we are tourists in our own country."

Interviewers: So, where's the life?

Lane: Ah. Chronicling. The chronicling, is a kind of returning to privacy.

Interviewers: Why?

Lane: It is the return to the original fiction of our lives which is our biography — where this whole interview started, which is to say, "we begin here, let me make something out of my imagination, which is at least real for me." If it is real for me it will be real for my neighbour, and if I can make it real for him, even though my neighbour recognises the fact that it isn't true, and it is also a song, then we can play. These small moments of enlightenment, these exquisite moments when we privately say, "yes" when we read a poem by someone you care about. In your own madness, God knows it is madness to turn to a poem at the best of times, to choose to find a thing that is not historical — because poems are not historical in spite of our attempts to make it all historical in our universities — to choose to find a moment that is exquisitely yourself out of the grand bizarre utterance that is language and say, "yes, this is me, here, now, at this moment, I feel this," and then have the arrogance to come out of that feeling and say "I've got a line here" and write a poem of your own, that is a wonderful moment. You've climbed out of the patterns and the rhythms and you've made your own.

The Physical Life:

The shadow of the Ambassador Bridge and the distant silhouettes across the Detroit River of abandoned skyscrapers and burned-out houses pose a surreal contrast to the beauty, power, mystery and vitality of the Maritime world found in the works of Alistair MacLeod. Yet it is here, in the shadow of the bridge, in a small corner office overlooking the quadrangle of the University of Windsor that Alistair MacLeod can usually be found. Since 1969 he has taught Canadian Literature and Creative Writing at the University.

As MacLeod is quick to point out, however, Windsor is not so far away from the physical working-class world of his Maritime stories. Like many of the Maritimers in his stories, the lure of work in the industrial heartland of Ontario has led to his physical, but not imaginative, removal from his ancestral seacoast.

One of the most acclaimed Maritime writers since E.J. Pratt was not born near the sea, but in North Battleford, Saskatchewan in 1936. During his formative years, however, his parents moved back to the family farm in Cape Breton where he attended St. Francis Xavier University before going on to graduate work at the University of New Brunswick and Notre Dame University. A meticulous, crafted writer, MacLeod's stories began to appear in American and Canadian magazines in the fifties and sixties, yet his output of books consists only of *The Lost Salt Gift of Blood* (1976), and *As Birds Bring Forth the Sun* (1986). This interview was conducted in Windsor on January 28, 1989.

Interviewers: *We thought we'd begin by asking an unavoidable question when it comes to your work: do you view yourself as a regional writer, and do you feel you've been stereotyped because you write about the Maritimes?*

MacLeod: Critics have accepted my work quite positively. The work travels very well or seems to travel very well — to the States, Norway, France. All literature comes from some place — some specific spot. Margaret Laurence's work comes from a specific spot, as does Mitchell's, the Brönte's, and Faulkner's.

Interviewers: Do you think the term "regional writer" is, therefore, a kind of phony term, a misnomer?

MacLeod: Some people see the term as meaning "small," while others would think of literature as coming from a definite region and going out into the larger world. Mordecai Richler is like this. Although he comes from Montreal, he doesn't write out of the total city of Montreal but out of a certain area of the city. Hardy was like that. Jane Austen was like that. The Bible is like that. Good literature, wherever it comes from, has universal qualities. If the work is good enough it will travel.

Interviewers: In your mind, what is it that makes something universal?

MacLeod: What makes things universal is that they touch a core, a storehouse of human experience and concerns that transcend regions and transcend time; such things as love between the sexes, or generation gap stories, or the awareness of betrayal, or death. These are stories that could take place anywhere, in any time. When the reader encounters these stories he or she responds, "Yes, I understand this."

Interviewers: The place you write about the most, the Maritimes, you originally encountered through stories. You did not visit the Maritimes until you were ten or eleven years old.

MacLeod: That's right.

Interviewers: When you first saw the Maritimes, how real had they been made to you through those stories?

MacLeod: They'd been made quite real to me. My mother and father were from the same community, and when they returned to Cape Breton from the West where they had been for a number of years, this was the community that had the strongest emotional hold on them. When I actually saw Cape Breton and the places and people they had described to me, they were just as I had imagined them. Looking back now, those stories must have been quite graphic and accurate.

Interviewers: Did you feel that Cape Breton was different from the West?

MacLeod: Oh yes. Very much so.

Interviewers: In what ways?

MacLeod: Cape Breton, like most of the Maritimes, has a very old historical tradition. What this may mean or what this does mean, is that people have been there a long time, generations upon generations — and this is true of Quebec but not true of other places where there has been a lot of assimilation — what this means is that if you go into any of those places in the Maritimes, you'll find that families have been there over two hundred years and their knowledge and memory of the place is generational. There's not that kind of mentality in the places that follow the resources — those towns that come and go overnight. There are no graveyards in the temporary towns. When you go through the Eastern Townships or the Maritimes by bus or train, you see these small towns with acres and acres of graveyards. Whereas, if you go into these new temporary towns, there are no graveyards because no one has been there long enough to die. My father was a miner, and he was following the boom and bust cycle of Alberta coal. The town that we left is half "vanished" now. Nothing but jackpines. No matter how hard it is in the "east," towns don't "vanish" in the same way.

Interviewers: Does the sense of place, then, come from the amount one has to remember about a locale?

MacLeod: One writes out of the material one has at hand, and memory is part of that material. The more memories you have — and memory is only one aspect of fiction — the more possibilities you have. It is like the amount of lumber you have dictates whether you build a hen house or a mansion.

Interviewers: As Faulkner said in The Paris Review *interview.*

MacLeod: Yes, he did say that, didn't he. I think that one of the things that happens with very young writers who do not come from a culture that is full of memory, is that their own memory is sometimes limited to their own lives. They only remember themselves. If they are seventeen, their own memory only goes back about a dozen years. If you have this cultural weight on your shoulders, your memory can go back into history. For instance, you may have been born in Toronto, but your parents are from Northern Ireland, and so you may still feel the weight of the turmoil there. So you are a very different kind of child than an "instant North American" who begins only with his memory.

Interviewers: People in the Maritimes, then, don't need to reinvent themselves in the way that most Canadians have to when they encounter the new experiences here.

MacLeod: That's right. No one in the Maritimes ever feels the need to reinvent themselves unless they go beyond the Ontario border.

Interviewers: When you write, how heavily do you rely on memory? You have that line in The Lost Salt Gift of Blood, *"There are only walls of memory touched restlessly by flickers of imagination."*

MacLeod: Oh, that's the character saying that. That's not me.

Interviewers: Okay, but how much do you rely on memory?

MacLeod: I think of a writer as someone who is reshaping things all the time, a kind of elaborate cook, who takes all these various ingredients and makes them into something new. Memory, imagination, an ear for dialogue — these are all the ingredients and you use them as you must to make things exciting and palatable. There was a brief time when I began to write, that people thought I was writing in an autobiographical way, or that. I was a confessional writer. This was probably because I use the first person a lot. But I am not writing autobiography. I just like to use the first person because it is effective. Sometimes, it has an intensity to it that I don't find in the third person. I have used the third person in three or four stories because the material suggests that use. The first story of mine that was circulated widely was "The Boat," and people kept coming up to me after its first publication, thinking that it was autobiographical, and saying to me "It was really too bad your father was washed overboard." You could say that those people are readers who are mistaking fiction for fact, but if you present things in a very detailed fashion, you are presenting the illusion of truth. Sometimes people cross over from the realm of disbelieving truth into the realm of absolute truth. I just think of that as the writer having done the job pretty well. One of the things that art says to an audience is "Do you believe me?" If it works, the audience says "Yes." I also think the reader has the right to say sometime, "Why am I reading this? What is there in this that engages my attention?" If the answer is "I don't find any reason to do this," then maybe the reader is justified in getting up and walking away. This doesn't mean a writer should pander to tastes, but he should say, "Listen to me, I want to tell you something," kind of like what an oral story-teller would do.

Interviewers: You always seem to make that clear at the beginning of stories, that you are telling a story.

MacLeod: That's right.

Interviewers: Is the oral tradition a way of keeping the past alive?

MacLeod: Yes, I think so. All stories happen in the past. No one as his house is burning down stands in the middle of it and relates the present.

Interviewers: Unless you are Jorge Luis Borges.

MacLeod: Yes. (Laughter).

Interviewers: It is almost as if you are moving characters to examine their own lineage and their own history — your stories often contain miniature histories of families and places.

MacLeod: One of the aspects of the Maritimes is that the people are a very old people, and that they've been there for a long time, and that people have been in some quite isolated places for a very long time. A large part of the Maritimes consists of geographical areas which are islands, and other areas are isolated as well. When you have a people who have been isolated in whatever region they've been in for two hundred years, almost whether they want to know these things or not they do. There are fourteen or sixteen black communities in Nova Scotia that have been there for well over two hundred years, and maybe the larger world of Canada doesn't even know they've been there, but *they* know they've been there. They know who their grandfather was, and who their great-grandfather was. They know these things.

And that's just common knowledge there. They carry that sense of history around with them without consciously thinking of it.

Interviewers: That sense of lineage, that is present in your work, and in the work of Maritime poets such as E.J. Pratt and George Eliot Clarke, tends to imply that the past is present today, that people tend to live with the past more easily.

MacLeod: It is that realisation that everyone comes from somewhere, that no one is instant, that everyone comes from their grandparents and parents. That is a kind of knowledge that each of us has. When we look inside ourselves, that echoes in our subconscious.

Interviewers: Language is very important in your work, obviously, but there's also a lot of non-verbal communication between your characters, and a lot of violence.

MacLeod: Just because people are not verbal does not mean they do not think, and it does not mean that very often they do no think and feel quite profoundly. I think that verbalising all the time is almost like another activity. More people can talk than write. By extension of the analogy, there are all kinds of people who think and feel who do not speak very much. I think this is especially true when you come from a place where your language is not like other people's language — such as the Gaelic speaking communities in the Maritimes. People who come to Toronto from Newfoundland, for example, are branded as peculiar or funny the moment they open their mouths. That means you keep your mouth shut because there's the built-in idea that these people will never understand you anyway. The argument from the other side is "I don't know what you're talking about." In the short story, "The Closing Down of Summer," one of the images I had, which seemed very foreign to the story, came to my mind from watching Howard Cossell interview basketball players of twenty years ago. There were these tremendous athletes who would do these ballet-like things on the court and then would be asked during a post-game interview "What was going through your mind as you were threading this basket?" They would always look at themselves on the replay as if they were art — which perhaps they were — and they would say, "Well, I just shoot the ball." What struck me was that they were doing more than just shooting the ball — they could do it but they couldn't talk about it. On the one hand you had an almost completely physical man in the athlete and on the other the interviewer who was sedentary and almost a completely verbal man. When I wrote that story, "The Closing Down of Summer," I asked myself, "What about people who don't talk very much but do splendid things with their bodies? And what if there are people who do splendid things with their bodies and no one sees them?" Another image I had in my mind, although it is not in the story, was the image of mountain climbers. These are world class athletes without fans. I was just very interested in the idea that all sorts of things happen in the world that are not verbal.

Interviewers: That non-verbal communication is almost tribal in the way you describe the miners on the beach in that story.

MacLeod: It probably is tribal.

Interviewers: It is a form of phatic communication.

MacLeod: That's right. I was interested in the fact that they represent people I know. You may find that same kind of tribal feeling among Italian bricklayers in Toronto. People in certain professions can do things within their professions without using spoken language.

Interviewers: Another example of the non-verbal gesture occurs at the end of "The Tuning of Perfection" when Carver brings the gift of whisky to Archibald.

MacLeod: Yes, that's all Carver can think of to do. Running through Carver's mind is the thought "I'll be a real class guy and show this man that I have class by giving him a gift even though he has lost the contest to me." But of course, Archibald doesn't drink so it is a useless gift. Archibald says "thank you very much" because he realises it is coming from a good heart and a good intention. As in "The Lost Salt Gift of Blood," gifts are very ambiguous. Sometimes you give the wrong things to people or give nothing at all, or the gift is misunderstood or left behind — that's what I was thinking of there. I tried not to have any villains in "The Tuning of Perfection." When opportunities come along, what may be an opportunity to one person may not be for another. So, there is no absolute right or wrong because it all depends on your vantage point. People sometimes have vision relative to where they stand. Some see a hundred-year-old family house as an opportunity to preserve the family heritage; others see it as a potentially great real-estate deal that will allow them to do all sorts of other things with their lives.

Interviewers: There are a lot of figures in your stories who do not want to trade their past, their culture or their language at any cost, and are determined to preserve it. You, in a way, are trying to do the same thing by writing those stories.

MacLeod: Perhaps. I don't set out to do that. I don't sit down and consciously say, "Here I go preserving the culture again this morning."

Interviewers: Is the Gaelic language very important to you?

MacLeod: I'm not very good at it. I can understand a bit. My wife can understand it very well. She writes it and reads it and sings it. What I find interesting about it is that I'm a sixth-generation Canadian and I'm the first person in my family who cannot speak the Gaelic language. I'm the first "to have lost it." Obviously, my children, who have a few words they've picked up around the house, will be in worse shape or better shape than I am. This is what the French Canadians are upset about — this feeling that there is something lost. It is not hard to be bilingual, but it is hard to be unilingual if you come from a place where the language of the past is not the language spoken everyday. It is hard to be a unilingual in one language to parents who are bilingual in the old and the new language.

Interviewers: Does place create culture or are beliefs and culture separate from place?

MacLeod: I think they all contribute very strongly one to the other. If you look at folksongs, if you look at the old ballads, they are filled with place names. If you come from any place where the natural world is quite strong, it is part of your culture, and it becomes part of your language. It is like the Inuit with their twenty-seven words for snow. Obviously, if they lived where there was no snow they wouldn't have even one word for snow. If you have a culture that's based on song or superstition — how to get across the stream or how to look at the moon or get across the snow — you use your language to adapt to the environment. In the case of the Inuit, their language and their place are very very close together and it is almost impossible to separate them.

Interviewers: Do you think the Scottish Gaelic culture adapted so well to the Maritimes because of the geographical similarities with the world the culture left behind?

MacLeod: What happened in Cape Breton was that when the majority of people went there, there was no one else around but themselves. In many ways, the Highlanders and the Acadians — those pockets of people you find in the Maritimes — were there for a long time and didn't intermix with other peoples, and this means a kind of intensification of culture in the same way you see an intensification of culture among the Appalachian people of West Virginia. They've maintained a kind of Elizabethan Scots-Irish language and culture there. There are accounts of Highlanders coming to the Hamilton/Dundas area of Ontario. You find mention of them in John Prebble's books. They wore kilts and certainly stood out, but because they came to an already highly populated and industrialised area, they very quickly assimilated and stopped wearing their kilts. Something is gained perhaps, and something is lost.

Interviewers: The people and the culture of Cape Breton that you write about began as a displaced people. Is that displacement key to their identity and to their perception of themselves?

MacLeod: It seems to be the contemporary problem for a lot of these people as it was historically. A lot of the moving on is caused by economic reasons. I guess all of Canada is made up of people who moved up and moved on for various reasons. This is part of the magic of the new country. A lot of the islands off the coast of Scotland where these Cape Bretoner's ancestors came from are now nearly unpopulated. Eigg, Muck, and Rhum, and Stikildec, for example, are so very underpopulated today that the British Army tests its secret weapons on one of them. If you look at a country like Scotland today, you find a nation where the newer generations are leaving. If you have ever been on those ferry boats which cross from Ireland to Liverpool, you see all those people leaving Ireland and crying. Why are they crying? Why aren't they glad to be going to their jobs in England? They're not glad. They're leaving because of necessity. Why did those six hundred thousand Québecois go down to New England to work in the textile mills? They could have stayed at home. They went down to make a living. What would have happened to Jack Kerouac if he had stayed in Quebec?

Interviewers: He ended up being very restless.

MacLeod: That's right. And that restlessness is still going on among the Newfoundlanders and the Cape Bretoners who go wherever the work might be — Toronto, Boston, wherever. In all of this, you have people who are forced by economic circumstances to spend their lives doing what they don't want to do in places where they don't want to be. This may or may not make for a kind of cultural schizophrenia.

Interviewers: Are you a victim of this cultural schizophrenia yourself?

MacLeod: No, not a victim, though I certainly carry a strong sense of history, a strong sense of place within me. I feel at home here in Windsor for I have lots of relatives here. This is one of the reasons why I originally came here, apart from the university, which is a very good place to work. Windsor/Detroit is full of Cape Breton people who came here to work in the auto industry.

Interviewers: In the story, "The Vastness of Dark," there is the feeling of the repetition of 'dispossession' — one generation following the other down into the mine until one generation breaks away and leaves the homeland.

MacLeod: I think that what happens to the narrator in that story is that he thinks leaving is simpler than it is. In his background there are people who say "it is terrible for you to go away from here," and others who say it will be wonderful. He thinks that leaving is the right choice, but once he becomes involved in it, it

is almost as if he doesn't have choice. It's like trying to forget your mother's maiden name, but you cannot do that.

Interviewers: It is something to do with the phrase you use in the story, "You cannot not know what you do know."

MacLeod: It is like people trying to pass for something they're not. What I was interested in with that story was the idea that people look at other people as clichés, but they are always rattled when they see themselves as part of a cliché.

Interviewers: The narrator is sitting in the car that has the Ontario license plate on it. Suddenly, you have a Cape Bretoner finding himself regarded as an Ontarian.

MacLeod: Yes, he's kind of disturbed by that. It is that whole idea of how we see ourselves as opposed to how others see us — to paraphrase Burns.

Interviewers: Your stories are filled with events that turn on their sense of uncertainty, and unpredictability.

MacLeod: Almost all my stories take place outside — in natural surroundings. The natural world is, of course, filled with uncertainty. Whenever anybody works in that natural world as a fisherman, or as a farmer, you spend a lot of your time looking at the sun, wondering if it is going to rain or not, or if it is going to hail or not. Any time you are engaged in the natural world, you are in an uncertain world. I'm interested in people who live their lives physically, because they are laying their bodies on the line. Anyone who is working in a logging camp, or a mine, or a fishing boat, is uncertain.

Interviewers: There are some certainties in your stories — for instance, the family house.

MacLeod: Sure, that's an environmental thing they can control.

Interviewers: *It seems that because of that sense of uncertainty, the characters tend to cling to certain rituals, especially superstitions and curses, for instance in the stories, "Vision," and "As Birds Bring Forth the Sun."*

MacLeod: I think the idea of the curse is a matter of peoples' pasts, of knowing things whether they want to know them or not. People live by what they know. For instance, if I were a haemophiliac, I'd live my life being afraid of cutting my finger. Or, it is like people who are adopted who spend their entire lives trying to find their real parents in order to explain things about themselves. They think, "If only I knew more about myself, I'd be happier." The danger, of course, is that they might find out things they don't want to know. It is like the Oedipus question. He says, "I want knowledge because knowledge will make me free." But the world blows up in his face. I'm fascinated by what knowledge will do. It is like religious rituals or charms — the idea of how you choose to live your life, how you can control certain things by acts of will which may override your knowledge, especially knowledge you don't want to have in the first place. Or sometimes, it is an intellectual control over an emotional matter, head over heart. In "Vision," I was really interested in that notion because that curse really happened in historical Scotland with such startling accuracy. Two generations later these things happened. Sir Walter Scott did write that poem. The thing is, was this really a prediction, or was it that these people had the prediction so heavily laid upon them that they just fulfilled it? The pull of information is very very strong — a curse functions almost like religious information and both predicts and explains the way things happen that we can't understand.

Interviewers: *Critics have pointed out that there is a lot of very graphic but not gratuitous violence in your stories, such as in "The Boat," "Vision," etc.*

MacLeod: I suppose, in the background of those stories I'm writing about the differences between someone who grows up in an urban background and someone who grows up in a rural background. In a rural landscape, you become accepting of violence, early on, such as even the necessary violence involved in slaughtering animals for food. Someone growing up in the city only relates to food as something under cellophane in Loblaws, and not as something that was alive and had to be killed in order to sustain life. I am, it is true, I guess, trying to ask some of my readers to face the fact that the natural world, and man's interrelation with it, often involves violence and what some may see as cruelty, and that it is still there in our twentieth century world.

Interviewers: *That comes out in the story, "In The Fall."*

MacLeod: In that story it is true. The man has to go away in order to work, and so leaves his wife behind for long periods of time. She has to look after his old horse while he's gone. So, it may seem on the one hand, when he sells his old faithful horse, that he is being cruel, or that on the other he is simply acting out of necessity. You can't choose sides in the story. But, you see, the children can't understand what's going on. They decide to choose sides and one of them goes and kills all the chickens in order to get back at the mother who has forced the father to sell the horse. It is like a child who can't stay up after ten o'clock and who throws his dessert on the floor in a tantrum. This does not solve any problems, but it is an emotional reaction to a hateful situation.

Interviewers: But the older son understands.

MacLeod: What I was trying to do with him was: as a child or as a protected person, you live in this world where you are surrounded by a kind of security. When that security is breached, you have to make a decision whether you are going to resist it and not understand it, or accept it and attempt to understand it and make the best of it. A sign of maturity is when you realise that you have to make choices even though they may be painful and unpleasant in their consequences for you personally. Sometimes the choice is made for you, by fate or by accident. But again, there, you have to deal with the consequences.

A Chance to Speak Differently:

Although she won the Governor General's Award for English Language Poetry, Erin Mouré's answering machine has a recorded message in French. She lives in a stone-fronted house, in a predominantly French-speaking neighbourhood of Montreal. Though born in Calgary in 1955 and raised in Vancouver, Mouré has chosen to live and work in Montreal. She works at the headquarters for Canadian National Railways. In effect, Mouré is, perhaps, one of Canada's most "transcontinental" poets, a fact that she herself acknowledges throughout her poetry, especially in the series "Seven Rail Poems" in *Wanted Alive*.

Mouré is a committed feminist, and many of her poems explore and debate feminist themes and issues, but always from an artistic perspective. We discovered as we talked with her, that she loves argument, and her method is Socratic and at times didactic, and always precisely logical in its process.

She has published six books of poetry to date. These include *Empire, York Street* (1979), *The Whisky Vigil* (1981), *Wanted Alive* (1983), *Domestic Fuel* (1985), *Furious* (1988, for which she won the Governor General's Award), and *WSW (West South West)* (1990). This interview was conducted on June 27, 1989, in Montreal.

Erin Mouré

Interviewers: *Do you think people got the point of what you were trying to accomplish in* Furious?

Mouré: The book was put together so that you can read it in various ways, so you can get various things out of it. There wasn't a "point" of accomplishment. The book's fourth section, "The Acts," is also its second section, because it is in a sense a set of "non-poems," complementing the three sections of poems. But on the other hand it is a set of prose poems, accompanying the three prior sections. I wrote "The Acts" as a kind of commentary on the poems, but it doesn't act as a commentary in the traditional sense. Sometimes the commentary key to a particular poem doesn't have anything to do with a particular poem at all! It has something to do with the impulse the poem came from, or with something I was thinking about at the same time I was writing the poem. Whenever you see two things in conjunction, there's a relationship between them, even if it doesn't appear at first. You can read the book as four sections of poems. Or, you can read the table of contents and the poems, and read the poems until you get a footnote and then refer to the "Act" which deals with the poem. Or you could read the Acts as a set of poetics, as some have, though I didn't particularly intend it that way.

Interviewers: Why did you use the title "The Acts" for that section?

Mouré: I used the title for two reasons. I wanted to challenge the idea that thinking is not an act — that there's action and then there's thinking. The two things to me always work together so that thinking is also an act. Thinking is an act, a process. The other reason is because in French, *les actes* means "the proceedings" as well as "the actions." So, if you think of the "minutes" of the poems, you have "the acts."

Interviewers: Ken Adachi took exception to something you said in "The Acts." You said "I don't want the inside of a poem to mean anything."

Mouré: I think many people are afraid of acknowledging there's so much in and of ourselves that doesn't make "sense," that doesn't "mean." People take exception to admitting something like that. But trying to make sense of things is already trying to suppress something. We've all got lots of things that are suppressed or repressed in ourselves. We like to make sense because it makes us less likely to jump off bridges and things.

Interviewers: Are you suggesting that there's an inside and an outside to the poem?

Mouré: Those terms don't have great meaning. By the inside, I mean what you've arrived at after picking the thing apart, so it makes "sense."

Interviewers: Why did you call the book Furious *and what were you "furious" about?*

Mouré: One of the meanings of "furious" is "intense."

Interviewers: Okay. In what sense?

Mouré: I think of furious as being intensity more than anything else, rather than anger. Though I suppose I'm just deflecting your question! Women have a lot to be "furious" about.

Interviewers: You dedicated the book to Gail Scott. What was her connection with it?

Mouré: Actually, I thanked her. She is a Quebec writer; it was she who challenged me to start thinking about what I was doing, and to stop pretending that critical thinking and poetic thinking were two different things, and that one was going to ruin the other. They occur at once.

Interviewers: There seems to be that union throughout Furious *of critical theory and poetry.*

Mouré: That is something I picked up secondarily, largely through Gail Scott, from the kinds of things that the writers of *la modernité* have been doing in Quebec, and specifically the feminist writers.

Interviewers: What argument from that have you picked up on?

Mouré: Well, it opened me up to the breakdown of the so-called "unitary subject" and of genres in post-modernist Quebecois writing, and the emergence of something called "the text." In short, in her book of essays, *Spaces Like Stairs*, Gail Scott says that in Quebec they've gone past the text; the novel is back! What attracts me is the idea of the thinking process *in* literature, that the writer is just not an observer commenting on things. In that context, you have to question the construct of your own self, and how the "self" is constructed in language.

Interviewers: There's the sense in your work that your poems are not meant to be objets d'art, but they are processes.

Mouré: Yes, definitely.

Interviewers: An ongoing process.

Mouré: "The text" has those kind of openings in it that I have picked up.

Interviewers: You quote Kathy Acker in the epigraph to the book.

Mouré: I've read a couple of her books and the quote I pulled out was one that cracked me up. Questioning language and the context in which to use language, and the way to use concepts, is not part of our process of "acculturisation." Her quote does that, and as such, talks about culture and failing. It spoke to me as a woman because culture has certainly failed women.

Interviewers: You suggest that this can be opposed by the notion of allowing women to inhabit both power and history. You say that you want "To inhabit freely the civic house of memory that I am kept out of."

Mouré: Being "allowed to inhabit" and "inhabiting freely" are not the same thing! That whole recognition has been important for women and women writers in various ways, because the whole idea of the city, the civic house, has been defined by men. The roles that women are assigned are defined by a system that nurtures and supports men. Even if women have complained about these things, the simple economics remain virtually unchanged. Women still, for instance, earn a little over sixty per cent of what a man earns. That's just economics, that's without touching at all deeper structures of language and thought! What I hope to achieve, what poetry in general can do, is challenge people to go off and think about things that affect them in a different way.

Interviewers: So you're not challenging them with reason per se.

Mouré: I've already said that pure reason is adulterated.

Interviewers: How did the "Pure Reason" poems in Furious *come about? Were they meant to be read as a set?*

Mouré: Well, the "Science" and "Femininity" poems were meant to be read as a set, because they are virtually the same poem. I had many poems, though, that for some reason I wanted to call "Pure Reason" because they examined the traditional ways of looking at things, and broke that apart. What I was saying in the poems was that I had to mock or even deconstruct the whole idea of pure reason because it doesn't make any sense. When I say "Pure reason is unreasonable," as soon as you have reason you are away from what is *pure* reason, so that any reasoning is probably unreasonable. The whole idea of reasonableness doesn't make any sense at all. It's a construct to batter people with, that's all.

Interviewers: Most of your books are divided up into sections that are almost like chapters.

Mouré: Well, they *are* like chapters. The method is common enough. I just can't conceive of a book that goes from beginning to end without sections! For my first three books, when I'd look at the poems that I'd written, I'd see what they had in common, and I'd throw out what was repetitive. With *Furious*, I consciously decided that I was going to write three sections of poetry with a section of commentary. The first section, "Pure Reason," I knew were going to be poems that were both deconstructing and reflecting more traditional ways of reasoning. The poems are disjointed, but in getting away from conventional habits of speaking, you can say more. I knew I was going to have a second section of love poems. The next section were what I call my ranting and raving poems — the fury of the book.

Interviewers: The poem "Rolling Motion," which begins the second section, seems different from the others. Was there a special effect you were striving for in that?

Mouré: Instead of using nouns and verbs to move the force of the poem I was using prepositions. The preposition is supposedly a relational term that needs other things to hang onto. It only has meaning in relation to other parts of speech; it is nothing by itself. I began to think of it as a kind of "women's term," playing the same role syntactically as women are largely given to play in the civic order. So, I was trying to push it to the point where it could act by itself. And ended up with the rolling rhythm in the poem.

Interviewers: You said in an essay in Poetry Canada Review *that nouns and verbs were a kind of male axis in language.*

Mouré: What language reflects in general, before you start thinking about nouns and verbs, has always been a male reality. If you look at the definition of the word feminine, you won't find the definition of Carolyn Osborne, body-builder. You'll find something else entirely. Yet she does embody the feminine, the "I am at home in my body" feminine, not the "my body is at your service" feminine. That's just one example, but there are lots of others. For women, the problem is how you are represented in language, in and by the structures and forces of language, without having any power or control over that representation. There is more at issue here than "history" or "power!" There are always constructs in language that have to be broken out of. For a simple example, there is the word poet, and then there is the word "poetess." Aren't women "poets?" Sure, the use of that word has largely disappeared, but the word "poet" still takes on the definition of a man who writes poetry. You never hear the term "male poet." But I have to say "woman poet!"

Interviewers: Is it the actual word or the meanings we've attached to it?

Mouré: Words are only the meanings we've attached to them. Otherwise they are just a bunch of sounds. There's no "actual word."

Interviewers: But there are philological origins for words. The word poet, for instance, means maker, and that carries no particular gender implication.

Mouré: It doesn't? In its philological origin, "maker" referred easily to women? Well, obviously something got lost somewhere. Seriously, that kind of "gender neutrality" doesn't stand up to scrutiny. When we say poet, we don't say "male poet" to refer to men. "Poet" already refers to "men." What I'm saying is that if we women exist in a language that doesn't represent us, and where we didn't invent the representation of us, then we have to look at where the worldly power of that language is, and disrupt it. Where are we always told the strong parts of language are? In the noun and the verb. Maybe if we "move" or dislodge those strengths, there's a chance to speak differently.

Interviewers: By using prepositions, for instance?

Mouré: Maybe. Women aren't going to be represented differently by use of the same order. But I'm not starting a new school of prepositional writing by throwing away the noun and the verb. All I'm saying is, if this is the way the order of language works and I don't see myself reflected in it then what is it that maintains the force of language? How can you disrupt that order and that force? What I end up saying near the end of "The Acts" is that as soon as you alter it, as soon as you move things around, it moves back again. You can't simply alter the force once and then go on and assume that the problem is solved. As soon as you tip the balance of the forces of language they assume a new balance. It is as simple as that. It is very similar to the old balance. It takes a continual act. You have to keep at it. There's no sort of "born-again" language that will save you. No single "act." Language is always going to reflect the dominant ideology, the way words are used, the way things have meaning, and the way things are either trivialised or hyperbolised in the civic order.

Interviewers: Does Furious *represent a new direction or a deeper direction for you?*

Mouré: Well, I think the central concern in all my poetry is the use of language, the relationship between speaking and writing and the body, and memory, and desire. Those kinds of things have always predominated — what we say, what we can't say, and what kind of manipulations occur in language. *Furious* is a very public, a very "civic" book. It addresses all these aspects of thinking. The newest book, *West South West*, explores voice, how it's possible for one person, one woman, to speak: the voice not just as articulation of a

"self" but as link with those others who inhabit us and whom we inhabit; and the way habits of speaking constrain us from realising those links: the relationality of it all. All this from a feminist standpoint. I think women more readily see the voice as polyvocal rather than constitutive of an "individual" only. *WSW* uses images of the West as well; the woman who says the West is inside her, the West as an inner kind of landscape. The West is not an outer kind of landscape that people can run around in. It is an inner landscape.

Interviewers: You were born in Calgary.

Mouré: I lived in the West until 1985.

Interviewers: How has the West influenced your perspective?

Mouré: I absorbed a lot of cultural influences from the West. Though I can't particularly separate them out from family influences. The images that I have, the ways I relate to other people in the world, obviously have a lot to do with my first relationships in that family, as everyone else's do. Mine happened to occur in the context of the West. A lot of people here in Montreal claim I have a Western sense of humour!

Interviewers: What would that be?

Mouré: I don't know. (Laughter). Most of my best friends at work are from Vancouver or Alberta, curiously. That dry climate, the environment, that area around Calgary where the mountains turn into the prairie, and spending a lot of time outside with my father and mother and brothers in that landscape: those things stay with me.

Interviewers: Do you see yourself as ever going back to the West to live?

Mouré: No, not right now.

Interviewers: *Is it a place of nostalgia, then?*

Mouré: No. I don't feel nostalgic about it. The images are very strong in me and they have relationships with other things I've encountered since, and are part of my inner constructs, by which I relate to the world. There's nothing in the West that I really miss; it's all inside me, even the smells.

Interviewers: *Your mother seems to have been an important figure. In your poems about her, your relationship with her tends to transcend the familial.*

Mouré: Other writers have talked about the mother too. And no wonder. Alice Miller, the psychologist, has talked about the sounds we absorb when we are in the womb. Through our mothers we get our first ideas of the world, and our earliest ideas of time and space. For men and women it is a really important connection, a possibility, which is mostly unrealised, the "mother" being such a social construct in this order. And I think daughters, especially, have to *deal* with that construct.

Interviewers: *You have the poem "Salt: Condition" which is about dreams. Do you draw on your dreams for your poetry?*

Mouré: Dreams give us ways of putting things together that we don't have in waking reality. When we're awake we're in overdrive relating to the world around us in a conventional way, for the most part. When I can remember my dreams, I like to think about their structures, and the events in them, and what their disjointedness means. Though I don't always mine dreams for poems, I like the way images work in them. "Released from the constraints of sensory order," as Israel Rosenfield says.

Interviewers: *Do you consider your dreams reasonable?*

Mouré: Nothing is reasonable. (Laughter).

Interviewers: *You've said previously in* Poetry Canada Review *that you are writing out of your body. When you lost the sensation of feeling in some of your fingers you felt a sense of loss.*

Mouré: I was talking about touch. Touch is something we take for granted — we almost don't consider it to be a sense. The skin is our largest organ. We don't consider that there is a relationship with touch in itself.

Interviewers: *You were also making the point in that* Poetry Canada Review *article that it was wrong for people to impose a separation between body and mind, and that it was all really one organism.*

Mouré: It is the same thing I was trying to say in "The Acts," where there are all kinds of processes that go into making acts, into thinking. Instead of looking at things from the point of view of the mind and the body, you can look at things from the point of view of attentiveness. We remember what we are attentive to. And when we dredge up memories of the same thing, we'll all remember differently because of differing attentiveness, and because people's inner constructs let them put different interpretations on the same event. There is bodily attentiveness, too. Your body is attentive all the time, otherwise you're in trouble. You lose your sense of self; it's bizarre. When I lost the feeling in those fingers I burned, I realised just how much our relationships to people depend on touch. The crossing of physical boundaries. We need that sense.

Interviewers: *Is that why you try to write for the sound? You've said that you use the sound of words as a texture because sound is as powerful a generator of meaning as what we call meaning?*

Mouré: Yes, words generate other words. The sounds themselves are the "meaning" by which we generate other words and sounds.

Interviewers: The body responds physically to sounds.

Mouré: Yes.

Interviewers: Such as the fact that Gregorian chant will stimulate endorphines in the brain.

Mouré: Sounds *mean.* There is a whole level of meaning that is based on sounds. All animals react on that level of language that has to do with sounds and rhythms. There's so much that's conveyed by sound and intonation but because we are so heavily into dictionary meanings we miss a great deal. Sounds carry a great deal of emotional meaning—so critical to attentiveness. If you were really attentive to sounds you would use a lot fewer words to convey the same thing. Even in a business context, if you don't pay attention to the sound of words you end up using a whole lot more words than you need. That's probably partly what "Bureaucratese" is. Inattentiveness.

Interviewers: You mention Bronwen Wallace in one of your poems. What aspects of her work do you admire?

Mouré: She takes the narrative voice that is almost, on the surface, a monotone voice, and she'll pick up the reverberations.

Interviewers: There's a difference between what she would describe as narrative and what you would describe as narrative. In "The Acts" you see your definition of narrative as differing from the traditional sense of the word.

Mouré: To me, narrative is what Gertrude Stein said: "Any one thing following any other." I don't view it simply as a plotted sequence of events. I think that sort of thing is restrictive of the definition of narrative. If you look at people like Oliver Sachs in his book about the man who mistook his wife for his hat, he says that we all have an inner narrative which we call our identity or our selfness, and it is something we can't see unless it has failed, as in the case of the man referred to in the book's title. Where narrative comes in there is that in order to remember how to get dressed and how to move around, the man would sing himself little songs about what he was doing. To compensate for the fact that neurological damage had destroyed his inner narrative he would make little narratives in the world. Without narrative he couldn't function. That inner narrative tells us who we are, why we aren't other people, and so on.

Interviewers: That seems to be the point behind Bronwen Wallace's poems.

Mouré: I think she tells the stories of women's lives and she consciously sets out to tell the stories of lives. I think the poems sometimes get away from that conscious pull in ways she doesn't realise, and she starts to bring in other things. For me, telling the story of someone's life, to me is like the idea of monotone narrative. Behind that, these little flickers come in of something else. The person's hands on the teacup become more important than the story she's relating. Other things start to enter into the poem and interrupt this person's history of their life so that...

Interviewers: So that our lives are the story of our lives.

Mouré: We can't tell it without getting interrupted and the interruptions to me are just as important as the rest of it. I keep working in and out of that personal world. You have to use it because it's what you "have." It is how you relate to the world—all discordant things fit together. *Furious* is a more public book than *West South West* in that it examines how language is used in a more public way, how language represents women as beings in a *public* order. *West South*

West looks at how the public order, landscape, the outer world, are concentrated in an individual. How in any case "individual" relies on "community" to speak itself at all.

Interviewers: *In your poem "Wearing the Map of Africa" in* Furious *you are making a very overtly political statement. What is the role of poetry in relation to politics for you?*

Mouré: The capital P "poem"? Language itself is ideology and dominance and oppression. As soon as you start to write a poem you can't start to unmix yourself up from politics. You can deny that it is there. Poems that say poetry is not political are usually just reinforcing the dominant order without questioning or acknowledging that it is there. In "Wearing the Map of Africa" the poem is about language and I talk mostly about the definitions of words.

Interviewers: *Like the word "calm."*

Mouré: Yes. In one person's mouth something that's occurring is a procession for the dead — a funeral. In the government's mind it's a riot. The poem is about language and about dominance. How can the word "calm" in this context mean anything other than oppression?

Interviewers: *So, is the poem a political act?*

Mouré: I think it is.

Interviewers: *There's a similar feeling in the poem "Villeneuve" in* Furious *where from "The Acts" you explain "the poem is not called 'terrorist' because 'terrorist' is a word conferred by those who have already taken power."*

Mouré: It doesn't work both ways, when Khaddafi calls Reagan a "terrorist," for example. In that case, it's propaganda, of course.

Interviewers: *"Miss Chatelaine" in* Furious *is also, in many ways, a political poem, is it not?*

Mouré: Well, it is a lot of things. It's a dream about a movie, or maybe an invention of a movie, about recollections of my childhood and adolescence, the unseen of that, about being able now to feel that I can talk to those women I grew up with, without having to worry about whether we passed or failed according to the definitions of femininity we were once so obsessed by, oppressed with. I know that in reality most of those women now are in their "secret marriages," that they are probably not feminists on the surface, but to me there is just a nice notion in the poem that maybe somehow we would be able to today get together and talk about feminism. Of course, feminism *is* "political;" it's a stance that doesn't accept the status quo.

Interviewers: *In many ways, today, feminism seems to be under attack, both from the left and the right; being perceived as having done too much or too little.*

Mouré: Yes. There has been a conservative backlash. "Feminism" to many people has had a pejorative sense to it. I've seen some women writers go to great pains to indicate that they are not feminists, even if they are writing a lot about female characters. I think that feminism is still disturbing to society and a lot of women included, because it doesn't just mean things like pay equity. It doesn't just mean things like women's control over their bodies and reproduction. It means looking at different ways of relating to people. How do we break down hierarchies so they stay broken down? I see, yet, some things that are feminist principles absorbed in different ways, even outside what people might categorise as "feminism." We still have to create mechanisms for listening to each other. We have to begin to get people to buy into getting rid of the paternalistic language and of authority and into new ways of doing things, saying things, before the opportunities opened up by and within feminism are absorbed and recuperated into the same order, the deadening order of commerce. And that's happening all the time, alas!

Getting On With Desire:

When we first met John Newlove in 1977, he was bearded, and wore a denim shirt and jeans to a reception at the Ontario Lieutenant-Governor's suite at Queen's Park in Toronto. During the course of that evening, while enjoying the company of fellow writers, he was an animated conversationalist, who poked fun at the ceremonial trappings of authority. Much to our surprise, when we met him twelve years later at his office in the Official Languages Bureau in Ottawa for this interview, we encountered a much different man. He was quieter, more philosophical, and his wit had become drier and much more subtle. He wore a double-breasted beige suit, floral tie, and cream-coloured shoes — every bit the summer uniform of a Federal civil servant. As we left the building on our way to do the interview, Newlove donned a panama hat and clutched a very British-looking black umbrella with a gesture of debonair flourish. As we crossed the streets between the office blocks, we could see the Peace Tower of Parliament Hill.

During the course of the conversation, Newlove spoke in a quiet, restrained voice, barely audible, as he slouched down in his chair, self-deprecating, shy, and evasive. But this posture was a mask for the intensity and philosophical verity of Newlove's ideas and statements. Behind the detached and formal civil servant is a passionate voice. When we asked him what had brought about the change since we last saw him, he replied: "I've learned to love again...though the marks desire made are still there."

John Newlove was born in Regina, Saskatchewan in 1938, and grew up in several small prairie towns including Verigin which is mentioned in several of his early poems. His books of poetry include *Grave Sirs* (1962), *Elephants Mothers and Others* (1963), *Moving In Alone* (1965), *Black Night Window* (1968), *The Cave* (1970), *Lies* (1972, for which he won the Governor General's Award for Poetry), *The Fat Man: Selected Poems 1962-*

John Newlove

1972 (1977), *The Green Plain* (1981) and *The Night the Dog Smiled* (1989). This interview was conducted in Ottawa on June 26, 1989.

Newlove: (Signing books). There's something about desecrating books that's rather attractive. (Laughter). Here we go. I have nothing to say except on technical matters. I remember once on the Gzowski Show he asked me how I went about writing a poem. I've thought about that for twenty-five years and I still don't have an answer.

Interviewers: That's a great way to start.

Newlove: We've got to start somewhere.

Interviewers: You grew up in the West in a town called Verigin, Saskatchewan.

Newlove: Well, actually I grew up in a bunch of Prairie towns. My mother was a travelling school teacher. I lived in Verigin for ten months or so, and then I lived in another town down the road called Kamsack, and that's what I called home.

Interviewers: The town of Verigin seems to turn up a lot in your early poems.

Newlove: Yeah, all that childhood stuff. Verigin is named after a leader of Doukobhors.

Interviewers: Your Kamsack and Verigin poems seem to deal with the coming of age.

Newlove: John Metcalf has told me I'm very evasive when it comes to writing. I think when I was growing up I was just copying things down emotionally. Even with all the violence it was like an earthly paradise to live there. But that's memory, isn't it?

Interviewers: That's what you talk about in the preface to The Green Plain *where you write: "it*

is so simple that I cannot describe it to you or myself. Thus, all these stumbling attempts to explain or atone. But it was a tangible vision of paradise. That paradise was broken, ruined abruptly after an eternity. I was Cain, the guilty one who did what he had to do. Is the mark on me? No. In the end, it was only, I suppose, a child's misunderstanding of the world and of himself. But these misunderstandings seem to stick. Most of what I write seems to go back eventually to that day; to the real knowledge of the existence of a veritable paradise and the real knowledge of the tiny monster, the ogre, lurking like a shadow in the greeness."*

Newlove: Yes. There seems to be something in a person when it turns out that paradise was not paradise that makes you think, very probably wrongly, that you were the person who spoiled the paradise. I know that can't be true but you seem to be the culprit for some reason. I don't know why. First I went to school and I tried to run away and they caught me. Something like that, I suppose, is so specious — delight in the sheer freedom of being young. What I remember, and I'm not sure, was that my mother was a teacher, and we lived in hotels. My memory of my childhood seems to me to have been very happy, though people have said it couldn't have been. It was like one long hot summer, playing in the dust with stray dogs. I had no responsibilities whatsoever. Nothing to do but have fun.

Interviewers: Looking back on that childhood, was there an actual event that separated you from that or was it simply the process of growing away?

Newlove: I don't know. I've never been able to work it out. Whatever it is, I've simply buried that under a lot of layers. Yes, I know what you're talking about, and the allusions to it in the preface to *The Green Plain,* but when I came to try to say what it was I couldn't. It wasn't that I couldn't say; I simply didn't know.

Interviewers: There seems to be a struggle in many of the Verigin poems where you are trying to comprehend violence but can't, such as the poems about drowning kittens in the rain barrel.

Newlove: Did you ever understand it? It seemed a natural thing to do, but why do it?

Interviewers: Or the massacre of the dogs?

Newlove: I remember my mother grabbing me and hauling me in when the shots were flying.

Interviewers: Was it that she didn't want you to see what was happening?

Newlove: (Laughter). No, no. I think she was afraid I'd get shot!

Interviewers: Earlier, you said that the poems up to a point were a kind of emotional note-taking.

Newlove: A poem like "Verigin Alone" is simply a shopping list of events.

Interviewers: By setting things down on paper were you trying to understand them better?

Newlove: I've always, as far as I can remember, been able to think better by writing things down. I can look at them and ask, is that true?

Interviewers: Margaret Atwood wrote an essay about your work, "How Do I Get Out of Here"....

Newlove: What a wonderful description she gave of herself. Not the description of me, but the attitude in which she wrote it. I remember, particularly, in one piece I wrote called "Public Library," she said it showed my Protestant hatred of the human body, or something like that. It is just a simple description of old men sitting around a library. What was it you were going to say?

Interviewers: Well, it was just that she seems to say that the emotional note-taking you were engaged in had boxed you into a corner.

Newlove: I don't feel I've boxed myself into a corner. I feel I'm standing somewhere outside watching the corner. (Laughter).

Interviewers: There's more to "Public Library" than observation, though.

Newlove: Yes. Insofar as religion is concerned, I was brought up as a very lax Anglican. I don't think Anglicans of my class had that sense of the world curiously bewildering but...(Newlove shrugs). *Nunc dimittis.* I don't really get religion.

Interviewers: But there's a number of your poems where you try to confront God or your feelings about him.

Newlove: Yes, *trying*. It is like when you are sixteen and you lie awake at night on your back in bed and you get up the courage to say "fuck you, Jesus." That's all there is to it. Nothing very important.

Interviewers: We had a discussion about this with Al Purdy.

Newlove: (Laughter). That's weird. Purdy's name just came to mind as I said that. And what did Al say to Jesus? You see, with Irving Layton, it would have been different because Irving would have claimed that he was Jesus. (Laughter).

Interviewers: There are some writers who feel their locales are, for them, places of refuge, like Patrick Lane in Saskatoon and...

Newlove: You know, Patrick is not from the Prairies. He's a convert.

Interviewers: Yeah, he's from B.C.

Newlove: You know, a funny thing, when I went back out West in 1980, I was sitting in the bar of the Hotel Saskatchewan in Regina, listening to people talk, and finding that I was disagreeing with almost everything they said. But I understood. I felt at home. It is just that simple emotional tie. You can go back.

Interviewers: *Do you think of yourself as a Prairie writer?*

Newlove: Absolutely. Well, not maybe a writer, but as a Prairie person.

Interviewers: *You have that poem "East From the Mountains" about remembering the mountains while you are in Saskatchewan.*

Newlove: Well, it's a very constructed piece isn't it. There's still something wrong with the last line, even now that it's twenty or twenty-five years old. Twice a year I still try to figure out a way to do the last line.

Interviewers: *The last line is "O tired and halting song."*

Newlove: I've got the rising tone and I'd wanted it to fall in tone so the poem ends on a sadder note.

Interviewers: *Some Prairie writers we've spoken to have said that they have gone to the Prairies because they lacked the sense of history, yet you've taken the opposite approach.*

Newlove: Wherever we are we can feel the ghosts all around us, the spirit of the tribes. If you can't maybe you should go someplace else.

Interviewers: *You mention the Indians.*

Newlove: That was the history that was all around us. As late as 1970, I remember moving to Toronto and walking around and wondering where were all the Indians?

Interviewers: *"The Pride" seems to suggest that for those living on the Prairies their real ancestors are the Indians.*

Newlove: In the sense that, as Wallace Stevens would suggest, you are your surroundings. It is a very simple idea that you are affected by your surroundings. There's nothing very deep about that. You'll notice with the poems about the Indians how constructed they are. The are almost theorising.

Interviewers: *And they are also very descriptive. They are almost like a history lesson.*

Newlove: There seems to be a way of doing simply by making a grocery list of facts, emotions and images, and commenting on them. Sometimes it is craftier to put the dish on the table and see if anyone comes.

Interviewers: *There's the same sense in "The Pride" as you have in "Samuel Hearne in Wintertime" …*

Newlove: But the Hearne piece is much better. In the Hearne there is not as much emotional manipulation as there is in the other Indian poems.

Interviewers: *Yes. Hearne seems to be watching everything, a witness, helpless. There's that moment when he's confronted by the Eskimo girl with the spear in her back.*

Newlove: The sense of helplessness. Frightening. The sense of helplessness that you write about so often because your own emotions are the same. The idea is that Hearne is supposed to be in charge, but he's not in charge. No one is in charge. This is poetry, not philosophy. I know we have to talk this way. The poem comes first. The theory afterwards. Certain critics, for their own obvious reasons, would have it the other way.

Interviewers: *Where do you draw the line between poetry and philosophy?*

Newlove: Don't know if I do.

Interviewers: *Because a poem like "White Philharmonic Novels" in* The Night the Dog Smiled, *for instance, reminds us of Rilke's "Duino Elegies."*

Newlove: Really? That's one of the nicest compliments I've ever been paid. I'm very careful, though, not to read Rilke too often.

Interviewers: *There's a sense in "White Philharmonic Novels," not only of emotional note-taking, but of trying to make some sort of understanding.*

Newlove: It is also the sense of looking at yourself looking. Of watching. Like Hearne. That poem was fun to write. You can imagine how putting it together was difficult because there were so many disparate elements. I was sitting there at the kitchen table writing it for so long and thinking I'm never going to get this right. Then you get one word that fits into place and you think, oh yes.

Interviewers: *How long did it take you to write it?*

Newlove: Outside of note-taking, and the reading and stuff connected with it, about three years.

Interviewers: *You've also pirated an amount of your own earlier work for the poem.*

Newlove: Oh yes. That's to put in a sense of déjà vu. The actual writing took about from August of one year to May or June of another year. That's not so long. It took Rilke ten years to do the "Duino Elegies," but he's not Rilke for nothing. What do you think of George Bowering's "Kerrisdale Elegies?" I

think they're quite nice. He's closer to the "Duino Elegies" there than I am.

Interviewers: *The figure of the outsider, the loner, comes up a lot in your poetry.*

Newlove: I prefer to say the observer. The loner has too much self-pity to it, and I'm rather too prone to self-pity.

Interviewers: *We asked because the poem of yours that is most famous in that vein is "The Fat Man." How did that poem come about? Was it an incident or someone you saw?*

Newlove: Exactly as it is in the poem. I saw the fat man standing at the corner with a bunch of carnations in his hand. Then I made up his paranoia for him.

Interviewers: *Because it seems to be a study of possibilities inherent in observation rather than just observation.*

Newlove: Yes. That's right. It is the sort of thing people do all the time — you see somebody on the street and you think about what their life might be like.

Interviewers: *But you take it further.*

Newlove: Of course. There's the pleasure of the rhetoric. There's the deliberately bad rhyming couplet, jarring ending.

Interviewers: *In some of your earlier poems you take a pretty dim view of women.*

Newlove: Well, of course you don't like what you haven't got. (Laughter).

Interviewers: *Was it really a matter of desire, then?*

Newlove: Yeah, it's that simple.

Interviewers: A lot of the poems seem to be tone studies on the matter of desire.

Newlove: Yeah, there's a lot about desire and the right desires to have.

Interviewers: Are the poems the product of desire or is desire simply the subject?

Newlove: That's a good question. I would say the product, but that's just guesswork. What they're the product of is that you get a beautiful sounding-phrase in your mind — it's a piece of investigation. It is a question of simultaneously standing back and being deeply involved, as if you are watching your own handwriting. You are deeply involved and you are also watching yourself being involved. It is a way of trying to think about things. It's like music.

Interviewers: It is like you are coming in to referee the thing.

Newlove: You are coming in to correct this thing. You have to watch whether you are lying or not, and you have to watch that it doesn't get too pretty.

Interviewers: You say in one of your essays you are writing for the ear and not the eye.

Newlove: Yeah. I guess a lot of people have said that your writing is bound within your own limitations. Of course, that's not true. When you write you're writing for the look as well as the sound.

Interviewers: But you haven't experimented very much with the look of a poem.

Newlove: That's true. I have done some experimental stuff, but first of all, I wasn't very good at it, and second I just wasn't interested. There's just so much other stuff to do. I've always had a dislike of anything of that sort in the arts — it seems to me there's a jealousy in

the arts of the sciences, so that in everything there has to be progress. This year's poem has to be better than last year's. I can see not only psychologically why it is useful, but also theoretically, why it is not useful to write a Shakespearean sonnet today, or to write concrete poetry. It doesn't really matter. What works works.

Interviewers: You have the poem "Shakespeare's Sonnets" in The Night the Dog Smiled.

Newlove: You'll notice that it is self-descriptive in its bounds. It doesn't have the same number of lines as a sonnet. Rather than ending with the couplet, the poem ends with the word "Us." It is a rejection of the metaphors, similes and philosophy of the sonnets.

Interviewers: When Margaret Atwood was writing about your poetry in the Seventies she said that what she saw as an affirmation in your poetry was a type of linguistic affirmation.

Newlove: Oh really? I often get this. For me, by and large, all my stuff is very affirmative, and not just linguistically. Which probably says something horrible about me. (Laughter).

Interviewers: But your more recent books, at least in the emotional sense, are more affirmative.

Newlove: Or maybe people are just getting used to it. Or perhaps more joy is present.

Interviewers: They seem to signal that you were in love again.

Newlove: Yes.

Interviewers: Why?

Newlove: If I knew I'd stop writing. Why, you ask me? Does this sound too dumb? I think as you grow older, Mother Nature anaesthetises you as far as the idea of death goes. I think you brood a lot more about it when you are younger, and you don't when you are older. I think, myself, that's one of the things. Perhaps I'm allowing myself to like myself a bit more than I used to.

Interviewers: Because there's that sense in the earlier poems where you seem to be saying "I don't want to die, I don't like myself."

Newlove: Exactly.

Interviewers: Later on you say in "The Permanent Tourist Comes Home" in The Night the Dog Smiled, *"I don't want to be buried in muck, so let's get on with life."*

Newlove: I think that's quite true. But it's not only that; it's the sheer ridiculous unfairness of life. It is a matter of deciding that it is okay to like yourself.

Interviewers: You don't want to play the Rimbaudian any more, the drunken poet off wandering the countryside. You have a very early poem about that, "Then If I Cease Desiring."

Newlove: Are you sure that's me? (Holds out his wrist). There's the crescent-shaped scar from "Four Small Scars." I guess that's me. The marks desire made are still there. About "Then If I Cease Desiring"? It's a simple statement. I'd gone off the drink. There's no literary allusions.

Interviewers: One poem that has a fairly disturbing tone to it is "What Do You Want?" — "I want a good lover / who will cook good meals / and listen respectfully; / shine my shoes, back my lies / with invented statistics at parties; / suffer indignities willingly / and be at my heels —"

Newlove: Well, it is a deliberately sarcastic piece. One of the difficulties I've had in reading it to audiences is that it has been taken literally. It was deliberately written in

a misogamistic tone to show what happens when you take the ultimate position.

Interviewers: You seem fascinated by dreams as in "The Pool." — "And in his dreams he came once to a clear sunken pool…"

Newlove: It's free stuff. "The Pool" is an unfinished poem as you can see by the last three or four lines. That part is so hurriedly tacked on.

Interviewers: Was it because you woke up at that point in the dream?

Newlove: Partly. And partly because I couldn't finish it. But it is very clear to me reading it that the last part is made up. It isn't part of the dream. As far as dreams are concerned, I like them not only for their randomness. I like the phrase "simple reality." I prefer to lie about and daydream. Other people prefer the simple realities.

Interviewers: In your most recent book, The Night the Dog Smiled, *you have a number of poems to or about poets.*

Newlove: Yes, I guess that's right. My affinity, of course, has always been for poetry, not poets. However, you are right. There are a couple, for instance, to Al Purdy. I do like his poetry, especially *Poems for All the Annettes* and *Caribou Horses.* The only thing he and I probably have in common is that we're both smart asses. I admire the kind of poem that makes me weep.

Interviewers: Do you aim for that with your own work?

Newlove: I wouldn't mind making people cry. Crying is a kind of recognition. It is when you understand the world and yourself that you are most deeply hurt. So is laughter a recognition. You have to be careful when writing poems because it is so easy in a poem to be an emotional bully because you know when the poem will work, so you have to know when to back off.

Interviewers: Can you give us an example of that?

Newlove: Yes, the one you mentioned earlier, "The Permanent Tourist Comes Home," which ends "Awkwardly, I am in love again." The word "awkwardly" is put in because it sounds awkward. It is that kind of flattening out, because how can you talk to strangers about your love for your dead parents because no matter what you do you are bullying them? It was written around the time of the death of my father, but it is really about my love for my mother. It is a very complex matter for which I didn't have any answers.

Interviewers: There's a split between what can be private and what can be public.

Newlove: Yes. That's the shameful thing about writing, isn't it? Because you have that need to tell, that need to talk. And the need to be loved.

Interviewers: And trying to reconcile the need to love with desire.

Newlove: Yes. Desire never ends. Do you think you ever come to a point in your life where you think you don't want to be loved anymore? Even by yourself? Desire is necessary but very dangerous. It is what separates you from despair.

Interviewers: How is it dangerous?

Newlove: Because it involves the desire for power, the vanity, the egotism.

Interviewers: At the same time you have to have empathy.

Newlove: You make yourself into what you are. It is not just the world making you into what you are. All writers I know complain about the lack of understanding, the lack of recognition, but at the same time to want that

hugging and approval just because you are a writer doesn't make sense. I don't know if it is possible to continue being a human being if you live with that kind of distorted desire. This constant appeal to a vast unknown public, to please, please love me, the idea that it is all right to be vicious and angry so people will like what you did....(pause).

Interviewers: After a while the writer becomes a sieve for the experience and what he writes about is what is left behind.

Newlove: Sure. Almost any writer who has ever lived is perfectly capable of moving himself outside of this.

Interviewers: But with all these people that you write about, the Indians, the fat man, and others, you were saying to the reader that we should love such characters.

Newlove: Perhaps, perhaps. For myself, still, the people I've tried to do that most for were the old men coughing away in the public libraries — the bewilderment.

Interviewers: You seem to identify with those men in the poem "Public Library."

Newlove: Yes, because that's how I thought I would turn out. I thought I'd be a raggedy-assed old man.

Interviewers: But instead you are a civil servant.

Newlove: I'm still dealing with language.

Interviewers: In what way?

Newlove: I correct government memos and edit a language magazine.

Interviewers: And that's it?

Newlove: Yep. That's life.

Getting There By Degrees:

On a cold, clear mid-winter day, we walked along the quiet Toronto Annex street to the door of Aviva Layton's house where Leon and Connie Rooke were staying while Leon served as Writer-in-Residence at the University of Toronto. As Connie opened the door, she kicked aside a pair of hockey skates. Leon was upstairs typing.

Connie showed us upstairs. We decided to do the photographs first, and Leon ushered us out through a second-floor window onto a flat, snow-covered roof where the three of us slipped and slid precariously toward the edge before deciding to retire inside to a safer and warmer location. He then explained that he was working on a play, an 'improv' called *Of Ice and Men*. "The play is about Harold Ballard and the Toronto Maple Leafs. It is all a bit foreign to me. I grew up in basketball country in the South. Canada's favourite pastime, I must say, is fascinating to me, but still very bewildering."

Born in 1934 in a small farming community in rural North Carolina, he was educated at Mars Hill College and at the University of North Carolina at Chapel Hill. He served in the U.S. Army in Alaska for two years, and was a Freedom Rider during the Civil Rights Movement of the Sixties before coming to Canada. He has worked at a variety of jobs, including that of a newspaper editor and a teacher of creative writing. He won the 1981 Canada-Australia Literary Prize, and the 1983 Governor General's Award for Fiction for *Shakespeare's Dog*. His published works include the collections of short stories *The Last One Home Sleeps in the Yellow Bed* (1968), *The Love Parlor* (1977), *The Broad Back of the Angel* (1977), *Cry Evil* (1980), *Death Suite* (1981), *The Birth Control King of The Upper Volta* (1982), *Sing Me No Love Songs I'll Say You No Prayers* (1984), *The Bolt of White Cloth* (1984), *Good Baby* (1990), *Happiness of Others* (1991), and *How I Saved the Province* (1991); and the novels *Vault* (1973), *Fat Woman* (1980), *Magician In Love* (1981), and *Shakespeare's Dog* (1982). He has also published four plays, *Evening Meeting of*

the *Club of Suicide, Krokodile, Sword/Play,* and *Cake-walk.* This interview was conducted in Toronto on January 26, 1985.

Interviewers: You've been published a lot since 1977. Does this represent a recent burst of creative activity or is it simply work that you've pulled together from your past?

Rooke: With rare exceptions it is all new work. There are about three short stories that date from an earlier time — "Mama Tuddi" would be one, "Sing Me No Love Songs I'll Say You No Prayers," would be another and there might be a third, but I can't think of it off-hand.

Interviewers: Do you feel any great pressure to produce work at a greater pace now, at the pace of a book a year you've kept up since 1979?

Rooke: The pressure is the pressure that comes from myself to complete anything that's begun. There's nothing so wonderful as to write that final page in a work and to reach that state of joy. That's what keeps generating work. There's no satisfaction quite like it.

Interviewers: It is easy enough to get started but another thing to finish something...

Rooke: Yes. I'm starting something all the time. Sometimes I start ten or twelve short stories at a time in a given day. I'll maybe write a paragraph or a page or several pages. At the moment, I must have fifty stories that I've begun that maybe went past those two or three pages and went on for ten or twelve pages, and then I'll hit a blind wall. But if there is any pressure, it is the pressure to slack off a bit, the outside pressure of people saying "you're publishing too much Rooke, too many books — we can't do a book a year." If there is any outside pressure it is the pressure saying slow down a little bit.

Interviewers: Isn't that good for you? It gives you the chance to keep the work in your hands longer to polish and consider...

Rooke: I could see how it could be. It might very well be that that is the case. But that's not something I really think about very much. I find that I work on each piece at its own pace. It is what the story demands that dictates the pace. If it wants to be written quickly there's not much I can do about it, except maybe leave the typewriter and go and trek across a mountain or something. One has to assume that it is a mistake to resist the impulse to complete. One must submit rather than act against it.

Interviewers: Has living in Canada affected your writing significantly? Do you see major differences between Americans and Canadians?

Rooke: No, I don't see any. I feel an estrangement from some things in the culture — for instance, hockey. I can go to a game and enjoy it but it does not touch me deeply. It is not something I know about like basketball or football. But when I'm writing about them — hockey or basketball or football don't matter that much. Someone else can supply all the information, the details. What is important is that you have to give the voice some range when you are writing about it.

Interviewers: What made you decide to come to Canada?

Rooke: There are two answers to that. One, I had just married Connie and she had just been offered a teaching position at Victoria. The other is that both of us had wanted to get out of the States. I never felt at home in the States. She, I think, perhaps did. But both of us had gone through the Civil Rights movement in the Sixties and I had been living in the South for a good length of time and it had become oppressive. I had never grown up with any of those native allegiances that you are expected to feel, that you are sometimes required to feel. I wanted to escape to someplace. My first trip to Mexico I thought I had come home. I felt so much more at home there. So the field had been worked long before the decision to leave the States was made. Canada beckoned simply because of the romantic sense of the unpolluted place, the uncorrupted place. There seemed to be a future up here that wasn't oppressed by dark clouds overhead.

Interviewers: You said that you were involved in the Civil Rights movement. Was that disillusioning, finally?

Rooke: Well, it wasn't disillusioning, finally, because, like all of those things, you start off with fifteen protesters and then you have two hundred protesters and that grows to thousands and it is a period when you are building, when the revolution is afoot, when you are saying "No, we'll no longer let you say to me, as a black, that I can't go and get a cup of coffee in your drug store or ride in the front half of the bus." So, it wasn't disillusioning in that sense. The numbers fighting for that equality and justice were continually building. But it was a terribly slow and tedious process, and it erodes one daily because just as one's own numbers are growing, one's counter-numbers are also increasing. It erodes one daily to fight that. It is a war and people begin to fall away daily because of terror or fatigue. It is disillusioning in that sense. But one feels rewarded because, in my case, one saw the blacks refusing to yield, refusing to submit, saying we have had it and by God we will have it even if it means we will destroy the nation in the process. I'm speaking mostly of my own little area where the war was being fought — but of course it was also being fought on a much broader stage with Martin Luther King and his wonderful inspirational messages leading us on. In the case of someone like myself who grew up in the South, it is a lifelong struggle. From one's childhood one grows up with it.

Interviewers: Were there early contacts with blacks that shaped your attitude when you were growing up?

Rooke: I grew up in a little town, Roanoke Rapids, North Carolina, where the blacks vastly outnumbered the whites — probably seventy-five percent of the people were blacks. I spent a long time at my grandfather's farm where we had many black neighbours and where we had many black workers who were living in little houses that we owned. There was a considerable degree of mixing between black and white kids. There was never any trouble. I had no idea there was any sort of racist policy at work on this small feudal estate or in the larger environs of the State or in the South. That condition of ignorance persisted pretty much up to my high school years. When I got to high school I realised there were no blacks. This seemed strange to me. The blacks, of course, were all over at the black high school. I was late coming to any sociological realisation of the reason for this. Somewhere in that period, during my blissful ignorance, some people were preserving and developing racist attitudes. Somehow, racist attitudes never hit me. I was aware of them, to some extent, in my home and among my neighbours, but I saw this as bizarre and eccentric behaviour that belonged exclusively to them rather than to society. It was only years later that it occurred to me that something was awry.

Interviewers: Was there that structure of established racism in the U.S. Army as well?

Rooke: When I served in the army there were blacks in my company and my squad. There was a lot of racism but there was also great camaraderie between blacks and whites. By that time I was clever enough to realise that this was the way the world moved and some of the racism in the army wasn't as nasty as it was outside.

Interviewers: You say you were brought up on your grandparents' farm. They were the products of the Reconstruction period. Did you find that their attitudes were influenced by that period?

Rooke: Not really, because people lived in very small pockets then. The farm was a pocket. Another pocket was the little store a couple of miles away. Our neighbours formed another pocket and then seven miles away was the little town of Roanoke Rapids. From time to time we went to town or crossed the lane to this or that neighbour's place but life in a sense was standing still. There wasn't a lot of interaction between one pocket and another because one worked eighteen hours a day on the farm and there was precious little social mixing.

Interviewers: It seems that your stories work on that principle — that people exist in those tiny pockets such as in "Bolt of White Cloth" or "Dream Lady" or "The Only Daughter" and Shakespeare's Dog. Is there a parallel between the fact that you spent your childhood in this situation and the fact that you keep returning to it in your stories?

Rooke: It hadn't struck me until you said that. I do that. My sense of time and use of it in fiction is largely determined by those years. On the other hand I think that although today's social fabric is different from the way it was then, life still continues on in pretty much the same way — we live in pockets. You know, people back in the old days didn't read that much. People on the farm certainly read the *Farmer's Almanac* and *The Bible*. But they listened to the radio so they had some idea of what life was like in New York. They heard shows from Radio City Music Hall. What was theatre? It was the "Jack Benny Show." Drama was "The Lone Ranger." And there were news flashes — someone would break in: "Berlin!" People thought, "Where's Berlin?" But then the Second World War came. Soldiers who found themselves in foreign countries were changed when they returned to America.

Interviewers: Is that what happened to your Uncle Donald?

Rooke: Yeah!

Interviewers: What was his influence on you?

Rooke: He was a maverick in our family. He was the black sheep. Most members of the family viewed him that way and because of that I was enamoured of him. I was moved by him and I learned from him. I was impressed by the possibility of being able to change one's direction in life. I liked his sense of the open sky. My first acknowledgement of the open sky developed out of my sense that he did not stay put but chose to move away from his closed environment. He was important to me for that.

Interviewers: Where precisely did Uncle Donald go?

Rooke: He went all over. He was very rarely home. He went to New York and California. I'm pretty sure he may even have gone to Montreal. But mostly it was just drifting from place to place. I think he just wanted a better idea of what the world was about. I think he was unhappy in his environment and gathered into himself a sense of wanderlust from somewhere. Probably he was just driven to do something like that because God knows there was nothing there in his own place for him. He did not want to be a farmer or work in a factory or run a shoe shop. He loved the fast life and had a gambler's instinct. He liked to drink and revel. He liked to be engaged in that dramatic side of life.

Interviewers: We understand you grew up in a one-parent household. It seems a lot of the children in your stories are children who have only one parent. Did you feel any sense of isolation as a result of this?

Rooke: It was something I was very much aware of and there was something very painful about it for a couple of years. I'm sure that situation does tie in quite a bit with the absence of one parent or another in many of my stories.

Interviewers: What did you do to compensate?

Rooke: I was more ingrown, more withdrawn than perhaps, your normal kid. It made me carry on silent conversations with myself.

Interviewers: With yourself rather than with imaginary playmates?

Rooke: Right.

Interviewers: Do you remember your father?

Rooke: I guess I must have been about two years old or so when I last lived with father. The next time I saw him, I guess, I was perhaps thirteen and that was only for five minutes, so I don't have a keen recollection of him. Those few memories that I do have are quite vivid.

Interviewers: It also sounds like he left the community.

Rooke: Yes, he was one of those people who never should have been married. He had a roving spirit. I'm sure that most of his flight from family life stemmed from an unwillingness to be imprisoned in a trap where he was powerless, that is to say if you were in that role you got out to the factory and you performed your job and brought your wages home and you bought a refrigerator. So, the rebellious spirit was a part of who he was even to the extent of wrecking other people's lives. Which do you put first? Your life or those other lives you care for? Which means the most to you? And it is a tricky point, because usually if you are going to stay there and be miserable you are going to wreck those lives anyway.

Interviewers: It seems to be something that is at work in "The Magician In Love", the idea that there is this roving spirit in Beabontha and the mother in "The Dirty Hells of the Fine Young Children." Is that perhaps a subconscious theme of yours?

Rooke: Some of these things I'm aware of and others I'm not. Why the woman in the "Dirty Heels" story left, I don't know. In writing that story I wanted to figure out why she left. The other characters toy with the idea — too much noise in the house. But I think I preferred not to know but I willingly accept the explanation that she left for the same reasons that my Uncle Donald left and my father left. Men were always doing that. But it is far more unusual for the woman to leave. If the woman did it, the explanation then usually was that she was a slut. There was more romanticism attached to the flight of the male than the flight of the female.

Interviewers: You seem uncomfortable with organised religion. You poke fun at Catholics and southern fundamentalists, radio reverends such as the lady in Sioux City in "Why The Heathens Are No More." What sort of religious upbringing did you have?

Rooke: Not much of any. There was a period when I was in my teens of about two years when I tried out the church. The church that was important to me for its theatrical value was the church heard over the radio, the old gospel hours and things like that, primarily because of the wonder of the delivery and the richness of the message and the bizarreness of the language and the wondrous singing heard from the black choirs. The reason in recent writing that I've been making these little charges at this or that body of religion and specifically at the evangelists is because I think they are a growing menace. On a recent trip down South there was scarcely a region that I didn't hit where I sensed that the evangelists hadn't been there before and were colouring people's lives and the way they think and act. It is a definite political menace. In the old days the local Baptist church was content to draw together several hundred dollars a month to send to the feeding of this or that mission in Africa, but their sights have risen considerably since that time. Someone like Jerry Falwell accepts the power of politics and they are now educating their children — they are not sending them to public schools or they are sending them to public schools and supplementing their education with their own message. Their education is being coloured. Religion is coming into everything. Not very far in the future the Moral Majority expects to have more students enrolled in their schools than in the regular public schools and they expect to elect more and more people to political office and they are doing so all the time. Do you think they are going to stop at the border? They are already here, but they are not working in Canada the way they are working in the States. They don't have hundreds of thousands of people on the phones yet in Canada.

Interviewers: We don't really have that fundamentalist tradition in Canada to a large extent, except maybe out West.

Rooke: Yes, except in the Prairies. It is a dangerous development. It is dangerous any time you get one body of people thinking and believing one idea.

Interviewers: It is interesting you say this because politics seems to be the missing subject in your works. It seems to be there under the surface, but it isn't there explicitly. Why is there this absence?

Rooke: You're right. This certainly hasn't been commented on or perhaps it is not even recognised. As I see it, my work is very heavily political. Reviewers will say that these are off-the-wall characters; these are not your mainstreeters. These are eccentrics outside of society. I don't see them that way. My work is political in the sense that it almost always allies itself with the underdog, with the oppressed, with those who cannot speak for themselves or who are not united simply because there is something about them that is a bit different. At

the same time, through the use of multiple voices, I see that as something that is political simply because it reminds us of the value of those distinct and truly different voices. I would say that these voices, these lives, however different they may be from the mainstream, are just as important as any other and perhaps more important because these are people who refuse to submit to political propaganda, whether that comes from some world-wide ministry run by the Moral Majority or from a government.

Interviewers: You seem to take a character at a point in their lives where they lack direction or come to realise that they lack direction. They come to a cross-roads where there is an external threat to something they want and they have to figure out how to get it or escape it. A lot of people today, when they get to that cross-roads, tend to turn to organised religion or a political movement. But in your work you are still putting the emphasis on the individual's choice.

Rooke: Yes. I see it that way. Certainly not all, but many of the characters I write about are really doing quite a wonderful job of their lives simply because they start off from scratch. They are in a hollowed-out tunnel, and their latitudes are few, their horizons are limited. There is not a great deal they can do with the lives they are given but within what they are given, they are doing an astonishing lot. The main thing they are doing is refusing to join the herd, and so they are concocting and putting together what I see as quite heroic lives simply because they are refusing to submit, to yield and if it means developing some sort of life which seems to be unworthy and of no import, then who are we to judge that? Usually who is judging that is someone who has started off from a much more elevated place in life, whose horizons are not fixed. Whereas my characters can't get any higher than that, they push themselves through the ceiling but that's not high enough.

Interviewers: Shakespeare in Shakespeare's Dog *appears to be the culmination in your work, so far, of an entrapped figure, maybe entrapped in the way your father and your Uncle Donald were in a small rural town and a demanding family life.*

Rooke: Yeah, there are little towns like Stratford all over England. Stratford was perhaps more wholesome than many in that it was a prosperous place. I don't think it matters much whether one escapes from these little places or not and the life and the drudgery in them, but it matters the way you perceive your own life. It matters that you perceive that. Yes, there is something you can do about the forces you are born under. A person does have the capacity to change and endure and escape.

Interviewers: Have you ever been to Stratford?

Rooke: I went to Stratford, I guess, four or five years before I started writing the book. I didn't go there with the idea that I was going to write the book. I was simply there as a tourist.

Interviewers: Shakespeare in Shakespeare's Dog *keeps on writing in the face of tremendous hostility in the environment around him and particularly from his family. It is never really explained what drives him to keep on doing that. Could you comment on this from your own experience?*

Rooke: I guess over the years as I became more committed to my writing and took more pleasure out of it, I began to have a sense of myself as one who would give most to life through it and could get most of life from it.

Interviewers: In Canadian Fiction Magazine's *biography of you, you say of the years between 1957 and 1964, "He tell no one what he do." Many writers have anonymous periods in their lives which are somehow formative for their later work. After that period was over did you experience a kind of rebirth?*

Rooke: Not a rebirth but more a sense of "Now I'm ready."

Interviewers: What during that period made you feel you were ready?

Rooke: Those were the years I was probably learning most about writing. Maybe I emerged from those years with a sense that I had begun to conquer technique or maybe with an easier and less restive sense of what my material was or was to be — my natural material. Maybe I emerged from it with a sense of knowing what I wanted to do with it.

Interviewers: What do you feel characterised your material up to that point that was somehow different afterwards?

Rooke: I suspect that during this period I wrote about fifty or sixty short stories. Most of those short stories were written overnight or in a short span of time. I probably sat down to each of them with the sense of "Boy, this is the most exciting thing in the world." But toward the end of that period, I probably said "Well, wait a minute now, it is happy and fine to sit and write these things in a great flush of emotion — you think they are wonderful as you are doing them, but what do you do with that sense that comes a week or two weeks later when you wonder what the excitement was all about?" At the end of those fifty tales I suspect I altered my sense of what story-writing was all about. I probably just adjusted my sense of what revision was and put less reliance on the flush of the moment. The honeymoon became shorter and not as static while in progress. I began to judge my work differently and to make different demands of it, and this altered, in a comprehensive way, my approach to the work.

Interviewers: In light of what you've just said, was "Brush Fire" a transitional work? You've said that there are autobiographical elements in it relating to the time when you were in the Army in Alaska.

Were you in a sense still too close to your material, still too involved in the emotional flush of it when writing that story? You seem to want to explain that story and justify the story much more than your later, more fable-like stories. "Brush Fire" is less symbolic in content than your later works and becomes straightforwardly didactic at the end.

Rooke: I was close to it, but not close to it in that it was autobiographical, although some of the incidents were true. It was autobiographical in the sense that I felt very close to that fellow Gode. I remember the ending of that story very well because it is an ending I've tried out in ten or twenty stories where I try to inject that kind of didacticism — but it usually winds up in the waste-basket. It is a technique that continues to interest me. I keep trying it with every third piece I write because I've never been able to do it the way I want to do it and to get from it the effect that I think is there in it. I don't know if I'll ever do it right. I'm most intrigued by the fact that I keep trying to use it, piece after piece, either at the end or some place else and I can't get in the work the kind of writing you find at the end of "Brush Fire." You see, "Brush Fire" was written during the Eisenhower years, dandelion years, when everything was covered up and covered over and puffed up and therefore more direct, hard-hitting statements were needed to cut through that.

Interviewers: Unlike the character of Gode in "Brush Fire" most of your characters are more down to earth, certainly not intellectual or academic…

Rooke: Yes. I think somewhere along the way I made a conscious choice to do this whether that was because of a recognition of where my own best talent was or whether it was a reaction against those writings that seem to say "Look how intelligent I am," I can't say.

Interviewers: Love is an ambivalent force in your works — sometimes it is positive and sometimes

negative and destructive as in Magician In Love where it is both the binding force that holds the community together and the power that drives it apart. Do you see it in these terms, that it is a double-edged sword?

Rooke: I think most often it is. I think that is the new reality, that love is both these things simultaneously — or if not simultaneously, one is certainly dead on the heels of the other. One of the things that makes love exciting is that it is like that. But one without the other, I think, is somehow fraudulent. We're not angels and we're not saints and that duality of doing good and evil comes with being human.

Interviewers: Is that why you put a sad ending on Magician In Love?

Rooke: I had a hard time with that ending. Probably because I didn't want to end it. Actually, I've done another forty or fifty pages on it and have just carried it on.

Interviewers: An extension of the work appeared in Descant *where the Magician's world continued, where the town was back together again, where everything hadn't fallen apart.*

Rooke: That's precisely because I don't believe in the ending of that book. It struck me as a tacked-on ending, an imposed ending. That piece in *Descant* is a curious piece. To this day I don't know where it could have gone instead.

Interviewers: Magician In Love *seems like* Fellini *does* Remembrance of Things Past *at* Thirty Acres!

Rooke: Yes! I do believe that's it! The thing that continues to attract me — and it gets back to where we started talking about life in a small town — I was attracted to that Magician and that small town because you know it is Winesburg, Ohio or it is Stratford-on-Avon in 1585, you can figure out or work out the lives that are at work in those small towns and I was especially intrigued with the Magician because he is such a powerful force in that town.

Interviewers: He creates illusions at will for people.

Rooke: And they blame him when what they do with those illusions goes astray.

Interviewers: You seem to be fascinated with someone who can create the illusion of reality. It is much the same as what the writer does, there's a sleight-of-hand to it.

Rooke: That is the case. I haven't figured out yet the power of that Magician on the people and what that means, their susceptibility, and the importance they attach to him — it remains something that baffles me. Why that willingness, in effect, to give your life over to somebody else? It is easy. You give your life over to someone else and then you are no longer responsible for it. I understand it in those terms.

Interviewers: After all, the Magician is human, he can't keep everything together, can he?

Rooke: Absolutely. He's experienced far more turmoil than most of the other characters simply because he carries within himself the power not just to pull rabbits out of the hat, but to change life, change things that have happened. For instance, Beabontha's husband comes to the Magician's house looking for Beabontha and she's standing right there in front of him and serves him a glass of wine. The husband doesn't even recognise her and the Magician has pulled off his wonderful trick.

Interviewers: How far can an author go with his own sense of the truth when he is creating a fiction?

Rooke: It remains to be seen. (Laughter).

Interviewers: Your female characters often, more than your male characters, are able to conjure up, almost in a manipulative way, a sense of illusion. The male characters tend to be entrapped or misled into accepting this kind of illusion, such as the relationship between Hathaway and Shakespeare in Shakespeare's Dog *and between* Great Garbo *and Adlai in "The Birth Control King of Upper Volta."*

Rooke: He thinks he's being quite charming. Also we see the Hathaway-Shakespeare relationship, a situation where they would have had a great relationship except for the fact that he is Shakespeare. Shakespeare liked being a father; he liked the security of the household and the marriage but he had to choose between this dynamite represented by Hathaway and his other love, the writing, which proved to be the stronger attraction. But had he not been Shakespeare, the way he was living would have been a good way to live.

Interviewers: In "The Deer Trails of Tzityonyana" the little girl in the story is another female character who while threatened by adults — at least the reader is quite fearful for her — is in control of the situation. She's confident that nothing terrible is going to happen.

Rooke: That's because she knows more than you know as a reader. She knows who the man in the car is and although she has never met the woman who he finally takes her to see, she knows who she is. The little girl knows that the woman is the man's new wife. The little girl doesn't know that the woman is blind, but her knowledge is much keener than the reader's knowledge, which is why she is able to retain the kind of control of which you speak. I suppose that kind of thing operates quite often in fiction where the characters often do know a great deal more than the reader. Adlai knows a lot more than we know. He's reluctant to admit that about the mother's funeral. We don't know what Adlai does. His response isn't our response. Unless you are depicting some utter realism, there is no reason why you should tell the reader everything. If the reader ever gets there, the reader gets there by degrees.

Interviewers: Isn't that unfair to the reader?

Rooke: You get to know a character in fiction the same way you get to know a person in real life. It takes a while. You don't walk into somebody's room and know instantly "Ah, this is who you are."

Interviewers: Yes, but you can probably meet that person again. You're not going to meet the character again even if you re-read and re-read the story.

Rooke: But by the time you get to the end of the story you've made some advances.

Interviewers: It seems that there is always some wonderful reversal of fortune for your characters at the end of each story, some sort of resolution of a problem. How do you know when you have an ending for a story?

Rooke: I'll tell you first of all that the story should not go along predictable lines. If the story goes along predictable lines, then I, as a reader, am not interested in reading it. As a reader I like to be surprised. If I know how a story is going to end, what is the point in reading it? You start out with the idea that you don't know where it is going or that there is something you've not yet understood about the character in the story and once you understand that, that will deliver you to some unexpected place. I'm not talking about manipulation at all — you have to be faithful to character. But if the writer delivers himself and gives himself over to the voices of the characters, then unless the character is a very humdrum character he is going to take you to that unexpected place. Take for instance one of the stories in the new collection *Bolt of White Cloth*,

"Sacks Fifth Avenue" — one of the reasons I was interested in writing that story was simply to find out why this guy was going on the way he was going on. When I finally got to that business about the kid in Peru and the fact that the man in the story is using some of his money he's being given to support these refugee children came as a total surprise to me. Now I have a choice as a writer once I reach that point. I can say "That doesn't make a lot of sense, does it? Peru? With this character? Why?" If I question it enough I can strike that solution. I don't set out to find the ending that will surprise some imaginary reader, but rather to let develop the ending that will surprise me. I like to give my characters some life after the story.

Interviewers: It seems that happiness and the search for it and the defence of it becomes the key issue in your work.

Rooke: I probably feel that way. I feel that way because "What is the struggle about? Why live a life?" One does not set out to live a life of misery. It is a reflection of a realistic appraisal of how most people conduct their lives. There has to be at least enough happiness in one's life to want to continue on, otherwise suicide...So that pursuit is a very real texture of people's lives. One measures the degree of that in one's life against the misery. If misery is greater than happiness, then you are in trouble. Some people, like the Fat Woman, get mileage out of small victories. She doesn't need anything monumental in her life in order to keep the struggle going. She needs little grace notes now and then even if she has to supply them herself. I think that goes on, even the sort of thing we're talking about, happiness versus misery. I think that applies even if you are writing surrealistic stuff or fantasy or whatever. Somehow it intrudes itself on the work. That's really what *The Magician In Love* is about — analysing the two and somehow wedding them together and being unable to put the ring on the finger.

The Telling of Stories:

Outcrops of sheer-cut rock, like high stone walls, lined the tracks of VIA Rail's approach to Kingston. On a grey February morning in 1988, our train from Toronto pulled into the station on the outskirts of town and we were met on the platform by Bronwen Wallace. "Before we head back to my place," she said, "I'll show you a bit of the city."

The way into Kingston was like the way into so many Ontario towns — the fast food franchises, the bargain outlets, the malls and stoplights. Here and there, the roadside was dotted by old buildings. Remnants of Georgian architecture still proudly protruded pillared porches around fanlight doorways. Then, she turned another corner. On the left was a building that resembled a Gothic castle with a fairy-tale gate. "That's where Clifford Olson lives." The towers of Kingston Penitentiary were cut from the same grey limestone that flanked the rail-line into the city. Not far away was the women's prison, and Queen's University, and as we drove through the downtown, the dome of the old government buildings rose stoically into the grey sky.

Bronwen slowed the car at the intersection of a residential street. "I used to live along there when I was a child. There's a poem about that. I went off looking for rainbows one day." "And now you're back?" one of us asked. "Yeah," she said with a smile. "It never really leaves you."

Bronwen Wallace was born in Kingston in 1945 and lived there with her son Jeremy. She published several books of poetry. Her first, *Marrying Into the Family / Bread and Chocolate* (1980) with Mary di Michele, was followed by *Signs of the Former Tenant* (1983), *Common Magic* (1985), *The Stubborn Particulars of Grace* (1987), and the postumous collection *Keep That Candle Burning Bright and Other Poems* (1991). She also published a collection of short stories, *People You'd Trust Your Life To* (1989). She won the National

Magazine Award, the Pat Lowther Award and the Du Maurier Award for Poetry. She died in Kingston in August 1989. This interview took place in Kingston on February 5, 1988.

Interviewers: The label "feminist writer" is applied to you many times. How do you react to that kind of label?

Wallace: Well, I am a feminist. I lead my life in a particular kind of way. I see the world in a particular kind of way — from a feminist perspective. By that I mean, a perspective which recognizes that our knowledge of ourselves as a species is incomplete until it includes the experience of women as part of our species-experience. I don't see that as a limitation, certainly, any more than someone like Pat Lane, who writes from a working class male experience is limited. In one sense, we are all limited by what we are. But I don't see my job as transcending those limitations; I'm interested in understanding, really clearly, what those limitations mean in terms of who we are.

Interviewers: In that case, when you sit down to write a poem, do you have to think about whether the message, feminist or otherwise, should predominate, or whether the original creative impulse should dominate. You have often said that it is a single image or memory that triggers the writing of a poem for you.

Wallace: I don't sit down and say, "Well, how can I make this into a feminist poem." That's just what I am. I don't think the poems would allow me to do that.

Interviewers: Some of your poems concern your son, Jeremy. He's obviously very important to you. Do you feel that your feminism has influenced the way he will look at the world?

Wallace: Actually, you'd probably get a better answer from him to that question but I think

he is certainly aware of relations between men and women as being political issues. I think he's really sensitive to that. I don't know how much I've had to do with that. He's had extremely positive male models in terms of his father and his stepfather. He also gets a certain amount of it from his peers at school who have been raised by politically sensitive parents. So there's a reinforcement of the sensitivity he gets from those of his own age. I asked Jeremy the other day, "Do you think you're different because your mother was a feminist," and he said, "I don't know any kids whose mothers aren't feminists in one way or another." He said he felt that feminism gives people control over their own lives and he felt that my feminism had given him control over his own life, and he feels he's had a lot of choices and had a lot of power.

Interviewers: Currently, a lot of commentators are suggesting that maybe feminism has gone too far in the past twenty years, that it has achieved certain political victories but at the same time has established new barriers between men and women. How do you respond to that?

Wallace: That's a hard question to answer because I don't see feminism as any one thing. Just as in any political movement, there are all different points of view; so too, there are many different types of feminists. I, myself, am not a separatist feminist, and I am alarmed sometimes by some of the more separatist stances that I see some feminists taking. On the other hand, I haven't been raped, I haven't been battered, I'm not a victim of incest. I don't feel the anger that grows from those experiences, directly, though I know it "collectively." In those areas, certainly, feminism hasn't gone far enough. I am much more concerned about career feminists who really don't want to change the structure of society to provide that women of all classes have equal access and equal power — Margaret Thatcherism, women who want to be bank presidents — I am much more alarmed about people co-opting the movement for their own ends. I don't see how Thatcherism changes anything for women. Gender doesn't make any difference in that case. Thatcher could be Mulroney.

Interviewers: But just the very fact that a woman like Thatcher can become Prime Minister has to say to other women 'these positions in society are now attainable for women.'

Wallace: Yes, that's quite true and maybe important but for me feminism doesn't just involve giving women the same kind of power that men have but giving women the kind of power we want to have.

Interviewers: Is that the central issue in feminism today?

Wallace: Well, I don't know. I don't think there is a central issue.

Interviewers: But maybe for you it is the central issue?

Wallace: For me, the concern is the difference between having power *over* other people and having power *to* do what you want to do or need to do.

Interviewers: Yes, you can see that in the poems which you have written about the clients of Interval House, the battered women, etc. Is the sort of power you are talking about the power which you, in the poems, wish for them — the power that comes from within that eventually allows them to get away from impossible situations?

Wallace: Yes, that's it exactly. There's a kind of continuum between all those situations in which power or violence is used to control people. I see it as a continuum between the man who beats his wife and the fact that we all live in a society where control is exercised by the use of cops or the armed forces who control how other countries operate. I wanted, in those poems, for people to see that the experience of the battered wife is not isolated from our experience — that the same power and violence is used against all of us. I want people to think about how to change their attitudes.

Interviewers: How did you originally become involved in Interval House and why did you leave there?

Wallace: I guess the answer is that all my life I'd always been very politically active. I was involved in student politics in the Sixties and the Labour movement in the Seventies and always involving women's stuff. Then there was a period, for about five years, when I looked after a friend who was dying of Hodgkins' disease. After she died, I realized that I wanted to get involved politically again but I wasn't sure how or in what. I really wasn't sure what the political situation was all about in Kingston. While I was trying to decide, I got a call from a woman who I had known all my life who had been brutally beaten by her husband — he'd gone after her with a hammer. It seemed to me that that was a message, so I started to work at Interval House. I had to leave because I was really allergic to cigarette smoke — you can imagine how much smoke there is in a crisis centre — and I couldn't physically stay there. Also, I couldn't do that kind of work and write at the same time.

Interviewers: You couldn't sit back and be reflective about your experiences there?

Wallace: At first I couldn't figure out why I couldn't write. I was working three twelve hour shifts with then three or four days off. A friend of mine who is also a writer, Isabel Huggan, pointed out to me that in order for me to write I have to be fairly open emotionally to where the poems took me, and then to go in that state to work in a crisis situation where I was also opened up emotionally, in another way, eventually became impossible.

Interviewers: Psychologically, were you becoming a victim of the violence you were hearing about?

Wallace: Well, it was more that there was no time to pull myself back emotionally.

Interviewers: What are the essential differences in creative approaches to writing between male and female writers?

Wallace: I think we have to be very, very careful about assuming that there are gender differences in the way men and women write that are genetic. I think there are differences in the way men and women write at this point in history, but I don't know whether they're genetic or because our social experiences are different. Therefore, my answer to that is that women are socially required to pay more attention to the everyday details, the minutae of how life is organized, of how conversation moves, or the nitty-gritty details of emotional exchanges. Women are socially required to do this in a way that men are not. I'm not saying that men can't do this. If I think of male writers I admire, such as Galway Kinnell or Philip Levine or Pat Lane, there is that same attention to everyday things. I like to think that it is social because I like to think that it can change.

Interviewers: You seem to approach your poetry through memory but it is not a memory in the past nor a memory in the present.

Wallace: I believe that at the centre of every experience is a mystery. The mystery, the wonder, whatever you want to call that, is immanent. It is not something which transcends the experience but is there in the

details of everyday life. That's what I'm interested in.

Interviewers: In one of your poems you say "My son is learning to invent himself." How does one do that?

Wallace: I think that we are constantly telling the story of our lives, and that we are constantly inventing and reinventing ourselves, and that has to do with the fact that our job here has to do with figuring out the mystery of our personality. That encompasses everything. A memory of something I had when I was five is going to be a different memory at seventy-five. The meaning of our life, and the meaning of each memory, unfolds as we go along.

Interviewers: Or, as Margaret Laurence says, we do keep changing our past.

Wallace: Memory is our past and we are continually reliving it all the time.

Interviewers: So the past is also our interpretation.

Wallace: Exactly. It is not fixed anymore than real history or official history is fixed. For instance, if you were to read the memoirs of a General at a battle in 1812, it would be very different from say the recollections of a soldier in the ranks. There's no one official history. History constantly changes and shifts.

Interviewers: But we're constantly trying to get at what really happened, what is the truth.

Wallace: I think that rather than trying to get at "the truth" we're all just constantly trying to figure out what something means.

Interviewers: You said "the poem is not an expression of emotion but a representation." What do you mean by that?

Wallace: What I mean is that writing a poem isn't a cathartic experience. I don't write to purge myself. I use a narrative form because what I hear in my head is a conversation.

Interviewers: It's a spoken intelligence behind the poems?

Wallace: Yes, in conversation we are always telling the story of our lives, always telling "what happened." But the other thing that is going on in my poems, is the voice of the speaker, the narrator, trying to figure our the *meaning* of "what happened," of the event. That movement, which is different from the simple narrative, is the movement of discovery, of mystery. That's what I try to do in my poems and I think people who read narrative poems just to find out what happened and not why something happened miss a great deal.

Interviewers: Are you trying to do the same thing in the short stories you are writing?

Wallace: I don't think I know enough about writing prose to know what I'm doing yet. In fact, at the Upper Canada Workshop I gave a talk and the topic of the talk was "Why I'll Never Write Short Stories." (Laughter). About six months after that people started literally talking inside my head, but I feel I'm still learning how to write prose.

Interviewers: What's the difference between your poetic voice and your everyday living voice?

Wallace: I think there's a real difference between my poetic voice and my everyday living voice...

Interviewers: For instance, there is not an alternative 'you' who is doing the speaking.

Wallace: I don't think the person who wrote any of those books is me, or at least me the way I am sitting here. There was a time in my life

when I used to get excited at the prospect of meeting a famous writer. But then I found a lot of these people were dull, were jerks. (Laughter). I thought, "Shit! How could these jerks write this beautiful stuff?" And when I started writing I realized that lots of times I'm a jerk, a total bumbling asshole, but I can still occasionally write a good poem. I think, for me, the way I resolved that, was that the poems come from this little circle of light I have inside me. I think that light is in writers, but I don't think that's all I am, and I think that's true for any creative effort. I mean, there can be a carpenter who can build beautiful things and also be a drunken fool. That drunken fool has that circle of light inside him when he's making a chair.

Interviewers: The experiences in your poems hint at events in your own life...do you order them?

Wallace: Oh yes, but a lot of that stuff is not my own life, either. I was very conscious of that in *Stubborn Particulars of Grace*. Clearly, there's a narrator who is not entirely me, who was on some journey of exploration, through what I find are four countries, represented by the four sections of the book. A lot of what happened in the poems did not happen directly to me.

Interviewers: There's a more cynical, bitter edge to the tone and the voice in Stubborn Particulars of Grace *that isn't there in your earlier works. The poems in the new volume seem more aphoristic. In "Change of Heart" you write "And I tell you / my need to believe this / is the closest I will ever come / to faith, that atmosphere / in which no one I know / can live, very long, anymore." There's a lot more of that kind of writing present in this volume compared to the previous ones.*

Wallace: I was reading a lot of Kinnell at the time I was writing that book. I was playing around with that because I sometimes kind of think that my poems go on too long, that I would like to be able to do the kind of thing that Roo Borson does so well — the short poem. I don't know if those lines always work for me. It is that aphoristic turn of phrase, lines laden with meaning in such an economical way. I want to do a line that will say so much.

Interviewers: Borson does a lot of summing up.

Wallace: Exactly. It would usually take me five or six lines to do what she does in one.

Interviewers: So what it comes down to is that you must decide whether you are going to be a poet of process or a poet of conclusion.

Wallace: Yes.

Interviewers: Most of your poems are about relationships between people — a lot of the poems are in a conversational form...

Wallace: That's true. I think the form comes out of conversations between myself and other women. It is not only conversations between women but in my experience it is mostly that. There is a kind of standing-back, a detachment, involved. Basically, it's gossip. It's gossip as an art form. Gossip looks at relationships and asks "what do they mean? What does the story about X mean to me?" So you stand back and you look at it.

Interviewers: Yes, and one can see that stance of standing-back in photography, for instance. You have indicated that the photography of Diane Arbus is very important to you.

Wallace: What I find really interesting about Arbus is that she had this reputation for taking pictures of freaks. But in fact, what she does is that she plays with that fine line between the freak and the normal. A lot of her freaks look

pretty normal to me and a lot of her normal people look like freaks. I find that fascinating. I love that line of hers "it's what I've never seen before that I recognize." I think there's a sort of guide in what she said, that element pulls me through the narratives in my poems. It is what I've never seen before that I will recognize on this journey. What I like about her photographs is that she catches people in that moment of intense mystery.

Interviewers: Yes, as you have said, you attempt to do that yourself. One can see that, for instance, in the poem "Appeal" where you speak of being caught in a moment of time at the supper table listening to your relatives tell stories. At the end of the poem, it is you recollecting them that catches them in a moment of time. You have become the story-teller.

Wallace: Yes. I'm telling that story, in the end, from the perspective of my mother and father whose age I've now become. I could not have written that poem a few years ago. Another poem I could not have written was "Fast Cars" where, at the end, again, I see things more from my father's perspective. When the narrator in the poem tells the story to a friend, she only talks about the boy, Doug, who she had a good time with. Later she remembers the story of the boy who went through the windshield. That's what I mean about how memory is constantly changing for us because we're constantly changing our sense of what life means. When she remembers the second boy, she has to put herself in a different position in relation to her father.

Interviewers: There's the same quality we're speaking of, the same byplay in the poem "One of the Things I Did Back Then." At first the narrator, when she remembers searching the birth records for the names of children who died at birth, remembers only that this information will be useful in helping Viet Nam War draft-dodgers get into Canada under an alias. But then, later, the narrator in the poem, in recollecting the incident, feels that there was a sense of violation involved in using those names in that way. The narrator thinks about the parents "of the babies whose names I stole."

Wallace: Exactly. That's why I bookended *Stubborn Particulars of Grace* with those two poems about prayer. I hope that what you see happening through the book is the narrator moving toward an understanding of the place of that kind of ritual in her parent's lives and in her own life.

Interviewers: *Stubborn Particulars of Grace seems to be a much more structured book, in general.*

Wallace: That's an interesting question because the first poems I wrote for that book were the Interval House poems. After that came the poem "Gifts", which is about my son. At some point, in beginning to write those poems that are in the first section I became aware that I was on some sort of journey of discovery. Halfway through the writing of what I saw at first as a collection of connected but not interconnected poems, I began to realize that they were really interconnected and the challenge for me was to show how interconnected they were. I was conscious of that when I decided on the order of the book. In fact, even in the writing of some of the poems I was conscious of that — this was a new experience for me. I worried in the past about being viewed as this single-minded narrative poet who just tells nice stories about her past.

Interviewers: *The image of striking a match keeps turning up throughout your poetry — about a dozen times or more. It seems to represent moments of revelation for you.*

Wallace: I'd never thought of it like that. It may be that it is simply connected with the fact that I used to smoke a lot. It has to do with a release of tension which you momentarily get when you light up. I think a lot of what I try to do is to invoke an atmosphere of as much familiarity as possible. To do that I have to go back to the touchstones of my own experience.

Interviewers: *Two of the most important themes in your poems are death and illness. You write, "Some people are a country and their deaths displace you", one of your most powerful lines. The deaths you talk about are not those of famous people, but rather, personal friends of yours.*

Wallace: Yes, as I mentioned, I was with a friend for five years who was dying of Hodgkin's disease. She was a very remarkable woman in that she was using her death as a way of teaching herself about how to lead her life. She taught me a lot about how I wanted to live my life. It sounds corny to say she changed my life but she did. Next to the birth of my son it is one of *the* major experiences in my life. It colours everything that I see or do — even today.

Interviewers: *In what ways?*

Wallace: I think what I learned from her the most is that we are all dying and that we are dying in all the ways that we are constantly changing and growing. When the three of us finish this interview this afternoon, that will be a death, that will be a loss. It won't ever happen again. Therefore, in this room with you, I want to be as completely and totally here as this is happening. Not so that I can hold on to it but so that I can let it go.

Interviewers: *Is that what grace is about?*

Wallace: Well, the grace that Pat gave me, through her death forced me to look at other people differently. I stopped being so judgmental, so them-and-us. I remember the day of Pat's funeral. I remember driving down the street and looking at all these people and thinking all these people are going to die. It was a recognition that all of them are living in this state of frailty. They were all trying to figure out the mystery of their lives as much as I was trying to figure out the mystery of my own life. That's what death gives to us, the chance to do that. I guess, in some of my best moments, such as in the last poem of that book, that recognition allows me to look at people with a certain...love, I guess. When it comes to death, we are all totally alone. It is something we have to face alone. But the other side of that is that we are all inextricably connected — we all have to figure it out. That's the kind of balance I try to get in my poems, that kind of shared ritual.

Interviewers: *And it really is the ritual that's important. In the first poem in* Stubborn Particulars of Grace, *"Appeal", it is not just the saying of grace that is ritually important, it is your father's joking about it afterwards, as well.*

Wallace: I think it is important for me, anyway, that I recognize that those spiritual realisations get worked out in a very hard and fast political reality. That's why the book is called *The Stubborn Particulars of Grace.* I continue to believe that people can change, that we can change what we are. A guy who goes around beating people up can become a guy who doesn't go around beating people up. But those changes are slow and difficult, they take place in the nitty-gritty context of *this* world, not some magic happening "after the revolution" or whatever. One of the things I learned from the Sixties, from living in communes, is that what really mattered was not a person's political orientation, but in the end whether they picked up their dirty socks from the middle of the living room floor. (Laughter).

Where the Arrow Falls:

David Wevill

The first thing is the heat. From the ceilings in most rooms hang large broad-bladed fans that turn slowly, moving the air slightly. History in Texas, according to Texans, began in 1836, but the hills opposite David Wevill's right-of-way to the Colorado River, just outside of Austin, predate Santa Anna's humiliation and the Alamo, with ancient limestone cliffs, with sidewinders, and vultures hovering overhead. We swam beneath huge spreading pecan trees and golden catfish brushed our toes as they moved lazily upstream toward one of LBJ's major political triumphs — the Mansfield Dam, an edifice almost as large as the gigantic monument to that President's ego, the LBJ Library. The temperature climbed to a dry thirty-seven degrees Celsius and a white glare from the afternoon sun hung over the hill country like an aureole.

The second thing is the dam. We watched a sailboat disappear into a fierce midsummer thunderstorm, and when the clouds passed no sign of the boat remained. Our shirts dried to our bodies as we drove back from the dam through the desert, and the desert was suddenly filled with flecks of bright flowers, brought to bloom instantaneously by the rain, then just as suddenly evapourated by the sun. This is a landscape where one treads cautiously, where beneath each step could wait a scorpion, a rattler or a black-widow spider. This is the country where Japanese-born, English-educated, Canadian poet, David Wevill has settled and it is like no other landscape encountered in Canadian writing.

Born in Yokohama in 1936, David Wevill was runner-up for the 1966 Governor General's Award for Poetry (won by Margaret Atwood). He is the author of *Birth of a Shark* (1964), *A Christ of the Ice-Floes* (1966), *Firebreak* (1968), *Where the Arrow Falls* (1974), *Other Names for the Heart: Selected Poems 1964-1985* (1985) and *Figure of Eight* (1987). Although he has lived in England (where he was a member of "The Group" during the Sixties), Japan, Burma, Spain and Texas, he remains a Canadian in his nationality and his spirit. He teaches English at the University of Texas in Austin. This interview was conducted near Austin, Texas on August 14, 1987.

Interviewers: You've been outside of Canada since the 1950's, but you've always made it clear that you regard yourself as a Canadian. What is your sense of yourself as a Canadian?

Wevill: I regard myself as a Canadian because I was born a Canadian, and because I grew up in Canada. I have very strong memories of that. Why I've lingered this long outside Canada I really can't say except that circumstances have dictated it. Barry Callaghan quotes Cortazar in *Exile*, "the only true exile is the writer who lives in his own country." But I think the other side of exile is one who never has a country, or who is not aware of having one whether he is in it or not.

Interviewers: The poems in Birth of a Shark *and* A Christ of the Ice Floes, *hearken back to those early years in Canada and to the Canadian environment.*

Wevill: I was much closer to the Canadian experience when I was younger. When I was in England, the thing that differentiated me from the others was being Canadian, having *that* background. Someone would walk up to me and say "How do you build a birch-bark canoe?" I think every young writer is trying to find his voice and his identity, his own range, to differentiate him from others. It is not an ego-need so much as a matter of voice. When I was in England in the early Sixties, there was Peter Porter who is Australian, writing poems about Australia, not as a nationalistic exercise, but simply to say "This is my past which is not your past." At that time I had no sense of when or whether I'd be going back to Canada. I had no sense of journey or return. I think, perhaps, that memory took me that way — I had to write about my past, not a nationalistic

past but a personal past. I was not writing for English readers or Canadian readers but simply to recall those people and things that were not present there in London or Cambridge.

Interviewers: The first line in all your book jacket biographies says that you were born in Yokohama, Japan.

Wevill: Well, my maternal grandfather was born in Prince Edward Island, went through various universities in North America, including the University of Toronto, and then went to Japan as a professor/missionary. He was there most of his life. My mother and her brothers and sisters were born in Japan. My father's family came from England. He went to Lower Canada College for a while and lived in Montreal. They moved out to Japan in 1912 because my grandfather was with Canadian Pacific Steamship Lines. So one side of the family was in place in Japan in 1912, while the other side had been there since 1896. My sister and I were born in Japan. My father was a businessman who moved back to Canada because of the war. The Japanese call that period the *"Kurai Tanima,"* "the black valley:" a time in the Thirties when there were all those political assassinations; when any liberal minister was in fear for his life. There was a growing influence of a group of extremely right-wing nationalist officers. Even as a child of about four years old, I felt a threat in the atmosphere. I heard the adults talking; I remember the fear in their words and their voices. My Japanese school friends and I were forbidden to play together, after a certain point. There were uniforms everywhere.

Interviewers: You turn to Japan and Japanese things creatively and philosophically in poems such as "Snow Country" which is based on Kawabata's book of the same title.

Wevill: Japan is a memory I've had all my life. On the whole, I was an isolated Anglo-

European child there, but I had Japanese school friends and I spoke both languages. It was quite a wrench coming out of that atmosphere to Canada and the Canadian school playgrounds with a lot of other refugee children, from England and other countries. This is a sense of exile, or difference, that has remained with me all my life. I'm not, for example, a Zen adept or a Japanese scholar, and I've forgotten all but a smattering of the language, but that beginning is something that I can't seem to outlive. When I am confronted with eastern thinking or philosophy or art it seems to be something very natural to me.

Interviewers: Have you ever gone back?

Wevill: No. Not as far as Japan. For two years I was in Burma.

Interviewers: Do you think those early years growing up in Japan influenced your poetry in any way?

Wevill: Yes, in subtle ways. Perhaps I want to draw and delineate images more clearly. The thing I admire about oriental poetry is the presence of space and silence. The presence of absence. That is something I'm not sure I've managed myself. The real effort is to make present something which is both silent and also soft-spoken, and the laconic genius in that. I still suffer from a dreadful need to want to fill things in, beyond the silence of their saying.

Interviewers: The oriental poet wants to build in silence as a feature of the poem, whereas the Anglo-Canadian poet always wants to break silence and to catalogue conclusively. There is that line in one of Leonard Cohen's poems about breaking the stoney silence on the seaway.

Wevill: This seems to me to be a factor of oppressive space, the need to cry out, communicate. I think Canada is a country where people want to shout, to be heard across a snowy field or glacier, be it city or tundra. Another poet might want to bridge that silence with an amplitude of voice. But I think in Canada a lot of the uncertainty comes from questions such as "Am I being heard?" or "Is anyone listening to me?" or "Is my voice audible?" I think much of the Canadian vitality and *angst* is the cry against space and silence—against oblivion. If we go too far out there into a snowy field we disappear or become wolves or bears.

Interviewers: Because you've been everywhere else but Canada for the past few decades — England, Burma, Texas, Spain — have you found it easier to deal with that awful, and ubiquitous question of Canadian identity?

Wevill: I think the whole question of Canadian identity is misleading. I think, for any writer, it has always been an ontological question, like "Will I wake up tomorrow morning?" The real question is more precarious than the question of national identity — "Will I survive, will we survive, will the earth survive us?" I've never felt the impulse to identify with any single country. Perhaps the closest I've gotten to a sense of native belonging was in Spain. But again, my *locus* there is an upland village, a place with its own precise intensities and conditions and laws. While I am not a native of this place, in time I have felt I understood something of the tremors of the local earth and the problems and conditions of the people I know there. But even that is not a resting place. One sees that and feels it and then wanders away from it and back to it. Something one *is* as well as something that one *is not*.

Interviewers: Was it at Cambridge that you first began to write poetry?

Wevill: When I was at Trinity College School at Port Hope, and in High School in Ottawa,

I did some writing. I started as a painter and I was determined I was going to be a painter — studio in Paris, etcetera. Then, when I was about sixteen, I became fascinated with poems. I think it was at Cambridge that the seriousness of the craft occurred to me. Craft, not creativity — they're different things. The critical atmosphere there was intense, and limiting. F.R. Leavis was still very much the touchstone, the oracle. The poetry was owlish, solemn, controlled.

Interviewers: How did you feel at Cambridge?

Wevill: Strange — at first. I felt I'd arrived at a cultural Mecca. People speaking perfect English sentences. Then, after a year, I began to resist this kind of perfection of English sentences. There was so much there, and also so much that was not admitted by the grammar and syntax of the place. I felt at home and also felt at sea. I've spent my life falling in and out of my own sense of belonging. It is not so much a sense of whether you belong in a particular place or milieu but a sense of whether it belongs in you. You are both the prisoner and the keeper of the keys — as were Mandelstam and Kafka, profoundly. If someone opens the door for you, you step in or you step out. If you are locked in a room that's another thing. I don't feel at *home* in Texas, yet I have a home here, children here. The community here in Austin is different from the rest of the state. It is a university town and the cultures mix here. It is both real and artificial. I live here both really and artificially, as a displaced person and a person placed by circumstance and need. If I had a country to represent, or a cause, I'd have said it by now. But I'm not from El Salvador, Poland or Ireland.

Interviewers: In your early poems you feel the need to place yourself somewhere, to have some sort of landscape with which to identify yourself. You have the line in "A Christ of the Ice Floes," "a man remaking himself in the image of March."

Wevill: That one comes also from direct memory. I had been back in Canada at the turn of winter toward early spring at the time my mother was dying in hospital. Also, I was born in March. I used to wander about in the Gatineau foothills. There is a connection with nature in that poem and that book which I think I've been losing steadily. At least referentially, there is a kind of connection to that boyhood landscape.

Interviewers: And your later poems are more philosophical, more interior, where you tend to externalise inner thoughts and feelings more.

Wevill: Yes. A kind of myopia has set in. Myopia or abstraction. I think in the early poems I saw things in more detail. When I was looking over the early poems for *Other Names for the Heart*, they struck me as being full of jostling images and details, things really compacted to the point where the poem sometimes contains too much.

Interviewers: In a brief statement you wrote for Contemporary Poets, *you say that you wanted to write "complete poems." What makes a poem complete for you?*

Wevill: Originally, I thought a poem should reach a finite conclusion. But I now feel that I want it to be more open-ended.

Interviewers: We ask that because Philip Hobsbaum wrote that you build up a poem image by image, almost to a complete stop, with a statement at the end. Do you feel when you are writing a poem that you are driving towards that point of closure?

Wevill: I'm always ignorant of where the poem will declare its ending.

Interviewers: The final line doesn't come to you before the other lines?

Wevill: I don't think that's ever happened to me. Usually what a poem starts with is the first line, and that comes from anywhere. Then it picks up matter as it goes along. I find it impossible to write a 'subject' poem. I seem to have to work some problem out and I address myself to that. Often, it goes haywire — the little imp, *duende* or desire, gets in there and says "no — stop — you think you're going ahead but you're going backwards or drifting sideways."

Interviewers: *You learned a great deal of your craft from contact with British, as well as Canadian poets. During the early Sixties, you were a member of the London-based, "The Group." Edward Lucie-Smith and Philip Hobsbaum stressed in their introduction to* The Group Anthology *that "The Group" was not ruled by a common style or ideology and that everyone was gathered from different poetic directions and different countries.*

Wevill: I'd have to agree.

Interviewers: *Yet the one connection you have carried with you from your days in "The Group" has been your friendship with Zulfikar Ghose, the Pakistani-British novelist who also teaches in the English Department at the University of Texas and who mentioned to us how he also felt out of place here.*

Wevill: Yes. Our both coming here was coincidental. He'd been in England longer than I had. When I came down from Cambridge to London in 1958 I was introduced to "The Group." But it was also in 1958 that I went to Burma, so I had only met with "The Group" six or seven times before I went away. By the time I got back, Philip Hobsbaum had gone and Edward Lucie-Smith had taken over. By that time, Zulfikar had come into "The Group." "The Group," at that point, was a magnet for certain young writers. It consisted of several young writers who had not yet

published a book. Most of us had been connected with Oxford or Cambridge. It was a good forum for working things out, for trying out new poems, new ideas and forms, and getting some sort of critical response.

Interviewers: *"The Group" appears to have been an international gathering. You were from Canada; Zulfikar Ghose was from Pakistan; Taner Baybars was from Cyprus; Peter Porter was from Australia; Edward Lucie-Smith from Jamaica; and George MacBeth from Scotland.*

Wevill: It never really struck me as an 'international gathering' in that sense. Everyone was aware of being a Londoner. I don't recall any discussion during "The Group" meetings of Australian or Canadian or Pakistani culture. It was assumed that London was the meeting ground.

Interviewers: *How did "The Group" work?*

Wevill: We met at Edward Lucie-Smith's house on Sydney Street. Poems would be submitted to him and then would get cycled out in sheets and mailed to various members of "The Group." We called them 'song sheets.' I remember that on a particular evening the work of one or at most two people would be discussed. About half a dozen pages of poems by a single person would be under discussion. After that there would be a free period when people who brought poems could read them aloud and we'd discuss them. On the whole, that was the way it worked. People took the sheets away with them, made annotations on them during the week and then brought them to the next meeting, drunk or sober.

Interviewers: *Several critics have suggested that there was such a thing as 'The Group poem.' Was there? Lucie-Smith and Hobsbaum suggested in their "Introduction" to* A Group Anthology *that the characteristics that all the members' poetry shared were that the poem was written in direct* *and natural speech; that there was a direct personal connection to the poem; and that there was an awareness of an audience for the poem.*

Wevill: I do think the poems came from personal experience and that they addressed themselves to the process of living, however small the specific experience or event. They were not literary poems, or at least not intentionally literary poems. Some of them seem that way in retrospect. I think there were poems that had to deal with people's childhoods and their current lives, and there were poems that dealt with events and current events. But there was no single *style* as those critics you've mentioned suggested. "The Group" was and will always remain a collection of individuals. If there were cross-fertilisations, it was the result of our encounters, nothing more.

Interviewers: You suddenly left London and went to Burma to teach for two years. How did that come about?

Wevill: Romanticism on my part. I was working in advertising that year in London, and one day I got word that there was a teaching job in Burma. So, I thought about it and decided I would go east and break away from London and the advertising world. I thought I'd go out there and confront the East in my past. I was immature, I was in love, and it seemed a big decision.

Interviewers: What was Burma like?

Wevill: It was intriguing. It was not at all a romantic time. Things there were intense and happening rapidly. It was a complex country to live in, in every way. I was teaching literature and history there. I found it challenging rather than exotic. Life there was vivid, vital and precarious. The British had gone from the country by that time as a governing force, but there was still a strong hangover, a British shadow overlaid in the Burmese *duende*. I got into difficulties there because I wasn't teaching English with the proper English accent. I was usually mistaken for an American. Good and bad results.

Interviewers: Did you try to put on a British accent just to keep them happy?

Wevill: (Laughter). No, I never mastered that. But there was a serious discussion about whether I should teach certain classes because of my accent. It wasn't *pukka*. Somewhere, between *The Waste Land* and Elvis Presley, the students understood me. I learned a great deal more than I ever taught them.

Interviewers: How did living in the jungle in Burma alter your ideas of what nature is? There's that comment of Michael Ondaatje's that Wordsworth would have had a very different idea of nature if he had lived in the tropics.

Wevill: Not jungle, but the northern end of the Burmese plain. It was a landscape that was both compelling and threatening. The life in the society was like that as well. Mandalay is set under mountains and hills on the east with the Irrawady River on the west. The jungle is further east and north up into the hills. In Burma you are faced with a wealth of both the familiar and the strange. I felt both isolated and at the same time part of everything around me. But I didn't write many poems about Burma, there or afterwards. That's the trouble with my life—a failure to record the immediate moment, experience. Trying to trawl through my memory at the same time as I'm taking in new things: the problem of pressure and absence at the same moment. While I'm there, in a place, I'm often elsewhere in spirit. I started to learn the Burmese language, and then I became interested in Japanese, the Japan I had not returned to in coming to Burma. In cultural or human relationships, this paves the road to Hell.

Interviewers: *After Burma, you went to Spain. What drew you there?*

Wevill: Apart from the poems of Lorca, Machado, Guillen, Alberti and other poets I had read, the first thing that drew me to Spain was when I was coming back on the ship from Burma and through the Mediterranean going back to England, and looking off the northern rail of the ship at the coast of what might have been Spain, I saw a high snow-covered line of mountains. I asked a man what they were and he said, "That is the Sierra Nevada of Spain." The words, the vision, stayed in my mind. I remember that particular moment. Then, in 1963, I went to Spain, and I fell into the place, as it were.

Interviewers: *You're on record, in a statement you made in* Contemporary Poets, *as saying that the thing you like about the Spanish poets is their terseness.*

Wevill: Yes, and their exactness. It is the exact record of emotion and experience, and a transformation of it at the same moment, which is rather like Ezra Pound's notion of the image. The image both transforms and records as it captures and alters an event. It seems to me that the best Spanish poets, in terms of thought and sensation and experience, do this very exactly. I think the reason for this is the sense that comes to you in Spain, that everything that is done is somehow necessary for life, however absurd it may seem at the time, however long it takes.

Interviewers: *Things are much more delineated?*

Wevill: Yes. So, if someone is sitting there all day long hammering at the sole of a shoe with great concentration, then he is doing something fundamental which I, personally, wouldn't have the patience to do. Among the Spanish there is this concentration on specific, non-projective action. This is deeply connected with how one is alive. The activity never reaches the point where it becomes abstract. They never ask what will follow this moment or what it will get them. They know that if they do it well, it has virtue, it is good.

Interviewers: *In the second to last section of* Other Names for the Heart, *you have the poems which you call "Rincones." What is a rincon, at least in terms of form?*

Wevill: A *rincon* is the inside corner of a room, a courtyard, et cetera. It can also refer to a place where someone habitually sits, say a beggar on a street corner, or a place where something notable happened. I also took the word *rincon* to mean a place in one's mind where memory lurks, where something is lit and identified. I'm not sure if it connects with the North American Indian notion of "strong place," a place of power, where spirits lurk. But that I take to be the sense of it. Those poems amounted to a book, but were never published as such. Each poem is a corner...

Interviewers: *We ask that because there's a strong sense running through your work of experiences and events being identified with specific places.*

Wevill: There's a desire to find a talisman to represent a place or time, although I'm not materially a collector. It is part of the sense of fragmentation of one's life that we take this thing from one place and that thing from another and conjoin, sometimes confuse, them. You're with someone and then she goes. You take this or that and try to hold on. You are always afraid of losing things, and yet you know that life is more or less all loss, though not always in a melancholic sense. One is afraid to gather or relate and yet one has to do it. It is of fundamental importance to yourself. Even in the act of doing, whether it is falling in love or into solitude, you see through it, beyond it.

Interviewers: *You have a poem where you say "There comes a time when the habit of moving on / overcomes the sense of being in any place."*

Wevill: As a child I felt it. Uncertainty. You find yourself sitting in a place long after the time you should have left. You become the statuary in the formal garden of your soul, a kind of Eliot aftermath. In a positive way, it means becoming like the Buddha. But in a negative way it means you wind up waiting for the bus that won't come.

Interviewers: *The whole question of obsession plays a major role in your poems, especially the later work.*

Wevill: Obsession is a condition inescapable for a poet. Some people wear this condition more lightly than others. Obsession can make or break your life. I've found I get pretty deeply drawn in. Relationships tend to become fundamental for me. It is ontological. There's a sense of rootedness, my root, the root of another. In a man and a woman it is like pair-bonding. The old Aristophanic notion of the self looking for its other half, which is blest by being almost impossible to find.

Interviewers: *"The hardest thing to imitate is yourself."*

Wevill: You quote me. Yes. Partly because yourself isn't really there. I think in almost all poetry yourself isn't really there. I think almost all poetry is about relationships, whether it is an intimate relationship or whether it is your relationship with the CN Tower or the passion between those two flies mating on the wall. Is there a bond between those two? Everything, as everyone says, is relative. It is a matter of how much you can catch with the eye, and finally, how much you can order that into a good poem, let alone a good life.

Interviewers: *When you write about relationships you are often writing about that sense of loss.*

Wevill: Rene Char said, "A poem is always married to someone." That should tell you where relationships end. You can be deeply involved with someone and at the same time see that person walking away, forever away, into the distance which is yourself. That's the odd thing about love poems — I don't think I've ever been able to write one, as such. I can't capture the moment, precisely or delicately. There's always that fear that comes in and says "you're fifty miles away from the one you love," and represents itself as a blank space.

Interviewers: *It has been said that of all the poets in* The New Poetry *anthology, your poetry is not violent but searching.*

Wevill: I've always been searching for something. I wish that, like Picasso, I would not only search but find.

Interviewers: *Throughout the poems there's a sense of wanting to confess one's sins of omission.*

Wevill: I don't like the notion of confessional poetry or of sins. I don't know what it means. It might mean something like St. John of the Cross, or Teresa of Avila. But I think you have to take that in a very strict sense because I think a confessional poet is someone who confesses to someone or something rather than simply confession about himself, an attitude of prayer. There are two poles involved: the confessor and the one who confesses. Confession implies a catharsis of sorts. That's why you must confess to something, to somebody. A prayer is heard. A confession is heard. The fault is either forgiven or not. But if you don't have a binary or bilateral situation then it is only someone crying out in pain. For me, I hope the form subsumes the content of the cry.

Interviewers: You have the lines in "Inktomni: A Prayer:" "There is so little to say that has not been said in better times. / We must reform ourselves against the contempt of things that knew our touch once. / I do not know if I have the tools to do it."

Wevill: That's an expression of failure, almost. A sense of not being alert or in touch. It is the same thing as "such and such took place and I was not there." This can build up into a psychosis. Inktomni, by the way, is a manifestation of the North American Indian trickster, as in Red Horn, in the first line of the poem.

Interviewers: But what you say about psychosis, isn't that part of the nature of art?

Wevill: It is. It is a question of failure *almost.*

Interviewers: If art refuses to admit its own failure then it somehow ceases to be art.

Wevill: Perhaps. It becomes a happy thing, a positive, projective, prospective light of the world. I sometimes feel that I've written nothing but elegies all my life. If that's the case, why? On the other hand, you can't walk away from it and say "I've reformed, I've changed my mind." What it comes down to is that you have to do what you can for somebody (yourself?) in terms of your own nature and capability. That is Zen. But the Christian attitude is you should actually sacrifice yourself for something or someone. We do that in any case without trying. It implies that you should lose yourself in another's need or another's life. This is an emotional truth. It is also hell on wheels. On the other hand, you are always in a dialogue with ghosts. The ghost is you.

Interviewers: Such as in the poem "Teacher" where you say your best friends are a dead wife and a living wife?

Wevill: Yes, helpfully or unhelpfully, the profound ghosts. At the same time you are dealing with the living ones whose selves you are. The living suffer me, I suffer them. One of the most important differences among poets is how present they themselves are within the poem. I admire poets who can put themselves, as names, fully within the poem, but it is something I find hard to do. To a degree, I'm present in my poetry as a combination of vowels, if nothing else. I don't think I could ever write a poem which began "This Friday morning, I, David Wevill, got out on the wrong side of the bed, kicked the cat, missed the toilet, pissed on my wife, missed her, wet my child..." (Laughter). There is a reticence in me not to push the poem in front of me as a four-letter word kind of shield. Yet I trust that there is a kind of x-ray effect, a see-through, where at least the *effect* of what happens *is* present.

Interviewers: Like a landscape of a dream? For instance, John Robert Colombo wrote that the primary influences on your early poetry were the worlds of dreams and dream psychology and surrealism, and that you had a grasp of them and how they worked.

Wevill: If that's true I think it is maybe negative capability. It is a subjection to dream rather than a manipulation of dream. I'm not a good interpreter of dreams. To me the edge is very fine. Events as we sit here and talk among ourselves — to what degree is that different from dreaming? I think we go to great lengths to offset the dream, to clothe the dream with the daily schedule at work, your wrist-watch, your trip on the subway. We're all trained to create a practical waking life as opposed to the dream life which is powerful and dangerous. Maybe this is the crux of the thing. I don't think, in the poems, there's a dividing line between the dream world and reality. I've driven a car for thirty years without even a minor accident. But when I sit down to balance a chequebook I might as well be reading cuneiform.

Interviewers: *Your interest in dreams seems to have led you to an interest in midwestern Indians, particularly in the poems of* Where the Arrow Falls.

Wevill: The title comes from a Persian story of the king who had three sons. He told his sons to shoot their arrows into the air and to build their palaces where the arrows fell. This worked all right for two of them. They built their palaces, married, and lived happily ever after. But the third one, his arrow disappeared, and to find it he had to go on a magical journey which involved ordeals. But when he accomplished it he had so much more than the rest of them. That was the title.

Interviewers: *Is what happened with that third son almost a metaphor for your own life?*

Wevill: Yes. Something like that. In an unheroic sense. I'm caught up in that kind of bewilderment. You don't know where it is going to take you. It is a kind of negative risk-taking, like a person who doesn't prepare for an archery match, who just walks up and says, let's see where the arrow falls. His virtue is his non-participation in the game. The rest is luck or fate.

The Permissible and the Possible:

Adele Wiseman

On one of those long rainy afternoons in November, we were in Windsor. We looked up Sunset Avenue (there was no sun to be seen) and there in the distance was Adele Wiseman, who was, at that time, Writer-in-Residence at the University of Windsor. She was carrying a load of laundry, and had her dog Oscar in tow. Rather than talk in the cold and austere surroundings of her office in the English Department, she invited us over for tea to her house on California Avenue (a street which bears no resemblance to its namesake).

The university administration had kept moving her from house to house, and she had not yet settled into the new location. Her tables were still wrapped in blankets, and cartons were piled in the corners. The first items she had unpacked were a number of strange-looking dolls and a large oval antique photograph of her mother — a portrait of a serious-looking woman in a head shawl, the penetrating eyes of which followed anyone who moved around the room. This was the mother who had sewn her daughter's 1956 Governor General's Award for Fiction into a collage wall-hanging of frolicking doll figures because, as she told Adele with the gravity of absolute playfulness, "Do you have any better use for it?"

Adele held up a clown doll, a clown modelled from her mother's memory of Barnum and Bailey's Circus tour of the Ukraine at some forgotten point in the last century. In its hands were tiny cymbals, simply brass buttons, waiting to be sounded again. "My mother," Wiseman informed us, "said that the dolls made her feel happy in her mind. I do a doll show, a sort of theatrical talk, with over two thousand of my mother's dolls. I try to show that the root of the creative process, before the intellectual thing takes over, is essentially psychological, that making things makes us happy, and I discuss the dolls in relation to any original act."

Adele Wiseman was born in Winnipeg in 1928, and was educated at the University of

Manitoba. She has published two novels, *The Sacrifice* (1956), and *Crackpot* (1974), the play *Testimonial Dinner* (1978), the children's book *Kenji and the Cricket* (1988), and a book about her mother's dolls, *Old Woman at Play* (1978). This interview was conducted in Windsor on November 3, 1990. Wiseman now lives in Toronto.

Interviewers: The immigrant experience is one of the major themes in your work. In your play, Testimonial Dinner, you make a distinction between the experience of Riel and Macdonald — two different versions of the immigrant experience. Could you elaborate on what the Riel experience means versus the Macdonald experience?

Wiseman: Macdonald interests me, in part, because he was a part of an immigrant group, like a lot of immigrant groups, who came here because they were kicked off their land back home. He did what so many people here do, just like our current Prime Minister; they forget things like the potato famine and learn from the oppressor — the successful taker. I read Creighton's two-volume biography of Macdonald. From the point of view of a writer, that book has marvelously slanted writing, so much so that nothing Macdonald did could be wrong. Whenever Macdonald did something wrong, Creighton took on a justifying voice. I found that fascinating, because, to me, Canada, like the rest of North and South America, has been founded by someone taking something away from someone else. James Reaney talks about the same thing in his play, *The Donnellys*. The taking away is my basic theme.

Interviewers: Grab or be grabbed?

Wiseman: Yeah. The be-grabbeds are always getting screwed. Now Riel, if you read about him, certainly seems to have been a very confused guy. For instance, he was hooked up

with the extreme right-wing clergy, the ultramontane. However, his experience, as a member of the Métis, propelled him into the idealistic religious camp, and from there, into an excessive idealism for what is possible for this country. Macdonald became the Queen's servant and the servant of those who in their orderly way were going to settle and rule the country — he was a pragmatist, and his nickname was "Old Tomorrow." His only mistake, historically, would appear to be his decision to hang Riel. The other thing about Macdonald is that he was a drunk. I think it is quite wonderful that we can refer to him in that way, whereas the Americans can't dare refer to George Washington without telling stories about cherry trees. Riel, on the other hand, had psychotic episodes, apparently, but was genuinely idealistic.

Interviewers: The point is, then, that they both had their own ways of fleeing reality.

Wiseman: Yes, but even with their faults, they represent our two possibilities. My point is, that we are way over toward the Macdonald side. In fact, we're now beyond Macdonald. Grab, grab, grab. The whole idea of Riel's caring, of caring for the native peoples, or of simply caring, is simply forgotten. We refuse to face the need for a way out of that either-or, Macdonald-Riel set of extremes, the possibility of a humane and civilised integration of the historic strains they represent. What *Testimonial Dinner* shows us is the intense pressures even on today's generation that continue from this dialectic. We're still being confronted with almost unbelievable negative choices that are not really choices at all.

Interviewers: In your novels, the two main characters, Abraham in The Sacrifice and Hoda in Crackpot are seemingly Riel types although Abraham certainly has Macdonald-like tendencies. Both seem to be pushed to the periphery, to the Riel world.

Wiseman: They are very much still immigrants, whereas in the play, *Testimonial Dinner*, there are three generations. Very clearly, one of the characters in the play is a grey "eminence" behind the throne — an advisor to the Prime Minister — and yet he is the offspring of immigrants. He's gone completely over to the Macdonald side. If you look at the history of the Jews in Europe, there is always a period of settling, of gradually making a contribution to a society, and then of being spit-out by that society. This is what this "eminence" doesn't appreciate: look, for example, at what happened to Mahler for years after the war. Whenever someone mentioned Wagner they would, in the same breath, denigrate Mahler. They would bring up his name just to make a negative comparison. The question of peripheralness is a truth — it can be modified, but it never changes.

Interviewers: So the question is of constant displacement. Do you still feel displaced because of your own background?

Wiseman: I don't know if it is a question of that. After all, I'm a writer, and it is my job to testify. Let us look at the three waves of Jewish immigration into Germany. The first wave, who came by invitation and included Mendelssohn's forbears, became assimilated. There was a second wave that was in the process of being assimilated when they were caught by Hitler — they still didn't really know who they were. The third wave were still the very visible immigrants. In that first wave, there weren't all that many and they were very highly placed. This was not the experience with the other two waves. The other waves were not wanted.

Interviewers: But you, as the daughter of an English-speaking Ukrainian Jewish mother, do you feel any process of transition that you have undergone yourself?

Wiseman: Yes. I think, in fact, I belong to both cultures. That's something that interests me very much now because when you're in my particular place you cannot look to any of the normal orthodox groups to find your home and feel, 'ah, this is my history.' You have to find with whom your peculiar evolution is linked, even if it is to other groups. Is there a link between other evolutions? I find I can trace myself back, though it is not familial but Judaic, to a long and honourable, indeed fascinating line of peripheries. Heinrich Heine and those later intellectuals who loved the language and culture of Germany, for instance, where they were born, and contributed enormously , were forcibly alienated, spewed out (if indeed, they managed to survive) and torn from their own sense of who they were. Eventually, after drifting through Paris and Europe, Heine came to the realisation that his cultural links were to the Hebrew poets of Spain, an earlier traumatised diaspora. Before he died he became a Jew again because he made a connection with another marginalised intelligensia, with his own real history. I guess, intellectually, I view that kind of thing as my line of descent as an artist. I have to know that I am a Canadian because I am. I have to know that I am a crypto-Christian because that was part of my schooling. I know a great deal more about being Christian than Christians can know, for instance, about being Jewish. But I am also aware of strong ongoing other realities, so you end up balanced on your toes.

Interviewers: Are public policies and programmes for the promotion of multi-culturalism increasing or reducing racial and cultural tension? In Memoirs of a Bookmolesting Childhood, *you have an essay in which you compare the Canadian Mosaic to the American Melting Pot.*

Wiseman: Yes. The question I'm posing there and which continues to agitate me is "are we really telling new immigrants that they are going to be allowed to function in terms of the societal values they bring along?" C'mon. It ain't true, I think. It is only true if you can use that as a way of holding them back. I can foresee some pretty sticky times. I can foresee a certain level of society, among the well-educated, mixing, and being able to deal with each other's attitudes. But in a world which has been so badly mismanaged that we are moving towards a horrendous Depression, someone else is going to have to bear the brunt of the tremendous frustration. The people in power are not the ones you can easily take out your frustration on — it is the ones who appear to be the usurpers that you'll take it out on.

Interviewers: What is the artist's part in trying to deal with this situation?

Wiseman: Well, the artist is the witness. It is a helluva thing to be a witness to murder.

Interviewers: Aside from the allusion to Prairie history in your Macdonald/Riel dialectic, and the fact that you are from Winnipeg, Eli Mandel says, in his essay "The Road to Wood Mountain," that you are a Prairie writer. You focus, however, not on the concept of broad space but on the idea of the urban community and your characters' relationship to it. Space tends to become inner space for you and your characters.

Wiseman: I've always felt that I carry the Prairie with me. I think most people do carry their landscapes with them, and make decisions in terms of those internal landscapes. For instance, people who come from the West Coast always come back to it, and that's partly because they are sort of cradled between the mountains and the sea. There's a kind of security to it, whereas the Prairie is expulsive. People don't go back to Winnipeg or the Prairie. Aside from the physical cold and the harshness of the place, it simply goes on and on, drawing you outwards.

Interviewers: Is Winnipeg still your spiritual centre?

Wiseman: Yes. I'll always know that I'm from Winnipeg. I really feel that the Prairie is internalised. When I go to Banff, I don't feel enclosed by the mountains as some people do. I perceive the mountains like in Rousseau's painting, "The Sleeping Gypsy," as if I'm surrounded by great sleeping animals. But, it is true that on the Prairies you can have this rather strange unsettling sense that if you go far enough you could fall off the edge of the world.

Interviewers: Yes, Abraham in The Sacrifice suddenly decides he's not going to go any further and that he wants off the train in a Prairie city like Winnipeg.

Wiseman: Yes, there's a sense in that of taking control of your own destiny, of not allowing space to control you. You see, a person like that, in that situation, has to in his own mind believe he is in touch with God or Moses or someone greater.

Interviewers: And there's the sense that you have to rationalise this decision because this is your homeland now.

Wiseman: You begin to believe in your own mind that you have been directed to do this. There's that sense also.

Interviewers: Even though part of the motivation for getting off the train is that Abraham wanted to save some money on his ticket.

Wiseman: Precisely, though that did not occur to him until after the decision. It helped to rationalise the decision.

Interviewers: One of the central questions in your work, especially in The Sacrifice, is "Do we accept the god that we are given or do we make our own God?"

Wiseman: Abraham tries to literalise what he has been given. The stories become immediate to him. Therefore, he is a character in the stories. If he sets up the circumstances correctly, God will reaffirm Himself by telling him. It is not only a question of accepting the God we are given, but of accepting him so completely that He is not a metaphor for Himself. What Abraham demanded of God was a degree of intimacy that, in our terms, is not realistic. You see, Abraham is very aware of the importance of ritual. For instance, when he substitutes as the *shoichet* he realises completely that in order to kill he must ask permission from God. He must apologise in advance. He must do it out of necessity. Polsky, on the other hand, does not have this sense. He is immune to the world of ritual. He deals with dead meat all day — he's a butcher. Obviously, when I have Abraham ritually sacrifice the calf early on in the novel, I am hoping that the reader picks up the resonance of the Biblical story of Abraham and Isaac, for I think that Biblical story is to be taken as marking, in that time, the end of human sacrifice amongst the Jews. This is a story that to a romantic, like Abraham, is something that he has to take very seriously. So, you see, despite his confusion sometimes he has a great deal of self-awareness. Abraham can't accept what God has allowed to happen, yet at the same time he feels bound to the traditions of obedience to God. In his confusion and need, he demands a personal confirmation of the covenant.

Interviewers: *On the other hand, Hoda in* Crackpot *does not seem to have the same level of self-awareness.*

Wiseman: *Crackpot* is, in part, a story about how a person becomes a strongly conscious self as opposed to being a not very strong self which her son exemplifies. Hoda has a strong personal myth. She has been given it in the intimacy of childhood even though it is a bizarre myth to everyone else around her.

Strange though she appears to be, she is, in a sense, more real than her son because her son has these fragmentary stories that come to him from outside but to which nothing in his real life has borne witness. In terms of personal intimacy the one woman he was close to, for instance, left him in a horrendous way. His sense of himself is very fragmented and open to being twisted from the outside, whereas Hoda's sense of herself has been forced into a kind of hermeticism that produces, to my mind, some of the more interesting deviations such as incest. How does the outside world look when you are not accepting the views of the outside world?

Interviewers: *So that's why, in a conventional sense, she may appear to be naïve, amoral, or immoral.*

Wiseman: She has a very strong value system, but it is a very different value system. In terms of what proper morality is, she has to come to it in the most primal way possible and the most difficult way possible. Most serious writers do find that they have to grapple with what is humanly possible at the point where it confronts societally, what is permissible. Their work re-examines the basic essences of our taboos. In one case, in *The Sacrifice*, I was dealing with murder, and in the other, in *Crackpot*, I was dealing primarily with incest. Both dance on the edge of that chasm between what is permissible and what is possible. I began by asking myself what is the best reason for doing the worst thing? That aspect of the novel is a kind of an enactment of that question.

Interviewers: *But when Hoda commits incest, it is not incest on the tragic level as you have in the story of Oedipus — there is almost an element of French farce about it.*

Wiseman: Well, how many plots are there? There are no implications because Hoda doesn't impose any, unless you perceive what she is going through. In the story of Oedipus, you have tragedy because they state before it happens that this is tragic, unwittingly tragic. There are no such conditions in *Crackpot*. It is made clear in the novel that Hoda is doing this not accidentally, nor for any perverse reason, though one could say it is a result of a whole series of her own choices, but simply to legitimise the maleness of her son. Hoda makes a moral choice; some would consider it a heroic choice; it is an informed choice, made with awareness. Hoda has become a conscious actor in her own life. Farce? Tragedy? You can name it. All I care about is that it reverberates with that haunting chord the reader can perceive as significant truth.

Interviewers: In Memoirs of a Bookmolesting Childhood *you make the distinction between acceptable facts and brute facts. You say, at one point, "brute facts are often the greatest lies" which is why you distrust newspapers. Is that, for you, the difference between fiction and non-fiction?*

Wiseman: Basically. There are different kinds of non-fiction. The non-fiction of newspapers uses facts to pervert facts, to pervert reality, and to confuse morality, as well. A journalistic truth can often be the worst lie, the most immoral lie, because it is made up of a careful selection of facts.

Interviewers: Because it purports to be absolute rather than variable?

Wiseman: Well, it is also selective, pointed. It works by implication. It does all kinds of things to truth that fiction can't afford. It can tell the sort of lie that fiction can't. Fiction can't afford not to be true to itself, if it is going to be good fiction. The most interesting thing is to analyse really good fiction in terms of where it is flawed, and you usually find it is flawed because of the journalising of its author.

If you read, in *Memoirs of a Bookmolesting Childhood*, the essay on *Portrait of a Lady* — Henry James was a wonderful writer and I wasn't really denigrating the book — there's always things that go click in your head and make you say, "hey." You have to take them under advisement because you have no one to talk to about them. I remember Margaret Laurence's copy of Milton's *Paradise Lost* was filled with pencillings: "Says who?!" She loved Milton, but he just got her into an absolute rage and she had nowhere to put it.

Interviewers: Further to that, on the topic of the use of fiction in Memoirs, *you say "I imagined that if enough of the truth were presented in a supremely obvious delightful story form the writers who were responsible for its presentation would, in very short order, redeem the entire world."*

Wiseman: Good fiction, to my mind, is both an examination and a judgment. The circumstances are not, strictly speaking, true. You make them up. But then, given the factors that are most highly relevant to fiction, such as voice, internal logic, your aim, both emotionally, intellectually, and every other way possible, is to produce a truth that is unassailable from as many different points of view as possible. If you do that, since you are examining, you are bearing witness, you are expressing a point of view, what I imagined is that you go from story to story you end up knowing how to behave, knowing what is best. I talked about my childhood. I assumed that because I had learned so much from stories that that was what stories were for.

Interviewers: That they were redeeming you from the world?

Wiseman: And potentially redeeming the world. If everybody had read and paid attention to stories, everyone would know how to behave. There were a lot of baddies around then, because not all the stories had been told.

There they were telling bad stories about me because I was a Jew. I grew up in a period when I was personally threatened because everyone else claimed that they didn't believe Hitler, but we, the Jews, believed Hitler. With a certain amount of megalomania, as a child, I believed that I had been born at that time to tell stories, and that if Joe Louis beat Max Schmelling, then we would go on to win the war and I could tell my stories. I believed there was justice in the universe.

Interviewers: Was there a particular event that made you want to become a writer, besides "Louis knocking Schmelling's block off?"

Wiseman: I always wanted to be a writer. I remember Daddy coming home from work and telling us stories. They were Biblical stories. He read the Bible all his life. I don't think he ever got out of it. He was always comparing himself to this or that character.

Interviewers: And you told stories to your brother to make him laugh.

Wiseman: Yes! Power! (Laughter).

Interviewers: You've said that something has to have textual density in order for it to be a work of art. What triggers that textual density for you and when do you know it is present in your own work?

Wiseman: I think it comes from a lot of reading, but it is a sense of purity of something suddenly being very concrete, and very specific. If the thing can be maintained, then you know the voice is part of it. It is not striking a false note. Also, a sense of largeness, not fragmentation, but a sense of no matter how small a piece you are dealing with the thing is whole. And, of course, the thing has to have an emotional intensity to it, there should also be a sense of urgency about it. Prose works in a reverse way from poetry; poetry is like the creation of the universe — it

is a contained explosion, always going off when you read it. A book like *Crackpot* creates the world of the poem in detail. Say the big bang is the poem and the unfolding of universes are the novels it set off.

Interviewers: What were the origins of Crackpot?

Wiseman: It is very interesting that you ask that. Certain things become obsessive as I carry them around in my head. Many years ago in New York, I happened to hear on the radio that little squib (epigraph) with which *Crackpot* eventually began about the Kabbalah. Call it the poem. I jotted it down because it really struck something in me, and then I lost it. I knew what it had said, generally. Then the character of Hoda started forcing herself out, and the quote just seemed to belong with the issues I was dealing with in the novel. As with a poet in a poem, you get two completely disparate ideas and something in you insists that they belong together. You sort of wait for something inside you to find the connection. As with *The Sacrifice*, there had been an actual murder in Manitoba when I was sixteen. An old Jewish man killed a woman he had been courting. She had been kind of leading him on. That summer I had been working at a fruit stall in the market, and the old man who owned the stall used to sit outside with his cronies and discuss this terrible shameful case. These are things that stayed with me. When I wrote *The Sacrifice*, I had actually written a story, which Malcolm Ross called the bare bones of a story, about two young boys, one of whom was obsessed with the Holocaust, and the fact that the SS men were supposed to have tattoos in their armpits. When they are in the shower together, the one who is obsessed sees the other's tattoo. Ross said that this story was just the bare twigs of the tree, and that it was not fleshed out. I went home and I felt and I felt and I felt, and I thought my way back to the question "who are these boys?" It turns out that the boys in *The Sacrifice* are quite different boys, but I had thought my way back to that particular story of the murder.

Interviewers: So the novels are a process of resolution for you between two things?

Wiseman: Yes. and an integration of all kinds of things.

Interviewers: You've written about that process of what you call "strenuous passivity," of learning to be patient in your writing, and not being in too much of a hurry to get something down on paper.

Wiseman: That's why I'm very careful about the whole workshopping idea. It is very good to get young writers working, but I've been around long enough to have seen a lot of good novels that could have been superb novels had the writers really examined some of the things they were writing about, and had they really got in touch with some of their obsessions. If they'd been in touch with them imaginatively, they would have been first rate. When I work here or in Banff I try to get people to take their time and look at what they're dealing with.

Interviewers: As you've described, that seems to be the way you worked on The Sacrifice. *Was it also true in the case of* Crackpot, *and was there any real-life model for Hoda?*

Wiseman: To begin with, the name Hoda is a variation of my own name. I really felt her pushing out of me. Among the many things that went into that novel, there is the memory of visiting home in Winnipeg, and spending the evening with old friends. One of them drove me back to my parent's house and I saw this silhouette of this very fat woman who looked vaguely familiar. Later, I realised she looked familiar because I had gone to kindergarten with a relative of hers. The man who was driving me said, "Oh, she's the local whore." Apparently, she did also look after an aged parent, like Hoda. But just that silhouette standing there, on the street, got tucked away somewhere. Just as with *The Sacrifice*, I did not want to know any more about what really happened. I stayed very much away from it. Years later, I heard that the lawyer who had defended the old man — and this old man was not unknown to my family, he had roomed with my aunt, was deaf, suffered from hardening of the arteries, was a widower — mentioned that he (the lawyer) was very annoyed with me because my story had nothing to do with what really happened. I said that's very interesting, because my story was not intended to have anything to do with what really happened. However, what did really happen to this old man was also a very interesting story. He had apparently given the woman he murdered his menorah as an earnest token of his intentions. She had taken it from him, and then laughed at him and turned him away. At the time I wrote *The Sacrifice*, however, I didn't want to know this story. It would have interfered with my reality.

Interviewers: And what was that reality?

Wiseman: The ending. It is the question I'm looking for. The world is full of answers. You just have to find the right question. I usually know the end of the story, but how does the character get there? What is the inevitable way that is going to happen? After all, fiction is art, not life. It is a made thing. The only thing, in terms of the story which is inevitable, is the ending. That's what seals it hermetically.

Interviewers: So, if the world is full of answers, it eventually comes and takes over a story.

Wiseman: Yes. Exactly.

Interviewers: You mentioned Margaret Laurence earlier. What influence did she have on your writing?

Wiseman: We knew each other from the beginning. She had graduated a year before me from United College, Winnipeg. We used each other as sounding boards for our work back and forth. By just talking a lot of things out we helped to clarify each other's ideas, in some sense.

Interviewers: *There's some sense of Hoda in Laurence's character of the snake woman in* The Diviners.

Wiseman: She read the first draft of *Crackpot* in 1969.

Interviewers: *About the time she was starting to think about* The Diviners.

Wiseman: I couldn't get it published. Eventually, I found a device which allowed me to shorten it by about fifty pages. It originally had a very rigid structure. I had been so enamoured by the idea of the architectonic, I had conceived *Crackpot* as two parallel stories: Hoda and her son. When you conceive something as a story of a strong character and a weak, in some sense, character, you're bound to have an imbalance. So, in that first version, there was a lot of the boy, his experiences, etc. Everybody who read it said that Hoda was more interesting than the boy. Actually, it was Margaret Atwood who had read it for Anansi, and she said something about this imbalance, and I remember standing at the sink washing dishes and being very resentful, and thinking they're all full of good advice. Then it struck me that she had said there might be a different way of doing it. Suddenly it occurred to me that if Hoda could hear about the boy through her uncle, then she would know where the boy was and what was happening to him, and so would we. And she could experience something I hadn't thought there would be room for me to deal with in the book — a kind of interpretation of being that is an experience I've had myself, just walking down the street and seeing someone and suddenly I know what it feels like to be that person. I was able to cut away a lot of the direct encounters between the reader and the boy and was able to tighten up the book considerably. I realise I'm not telling you a whole lot about Laurence here (Laughter).

Interviewers: *You, in* The Sacrifice, *and Laurence, in* The Diviners, *seem to be searching for a myth that is central to your respective cultures.*

Wiseman: Well, you see she did see herself as part of a displaced nation. One of the interesting things about Margaret Laurence is that she, in her own family, was Lowland Scots. Her original name was Margaret Wemyss. But her husband, Jack, was a Highlander. Margaret was very much moved by the stories of the Clearances. It was a way in which she and I connected, both displaced people.

Interviewers: *The sense of coming from cultures which had experienced diaspores?*

Wiseman: Yes, and she saw that everyone in Canada was displaced.

Interviewers: *You were very young when you began* The Sacrifice. *Were you trying to write your past out of you as young authors are prone to do? How much of your own past was in that novel?*

Wiseman: Not much. There's only one fiction story that I would say is autobiographical, "On Wings of Tongue." It is the only thing I've ever written that is autobiographical in essence. The woman who was the basis for Mrs. Lemon was a lady who lived with us. She would go from one family to another, rush off, and then beg to come back. I always wanted to go and visit her in the Selkirk mental hospital, but I never did.

She was very generous. She would go to the store and buy us candy with her relief tickets. None of my other works are as close as that story because I always thought that if you are a writer you are supposed to make things up. That's the other reason why I'm such a slow writer.

Interviewers: There must have been quite a bit of pressure on you, though, to produce another work rather quickly after you won the Governor General's Award for your first book, The Sacrifice.

Wiseman: Yes, there was, but I had this notion of writing as a pure vocation, and I wasn't out to sell my purpose by embarking on something I didn't want to do. I remember having a conversation with Margaret Laurence very early on about what we'd do if we won the Governor General's Award. I've watched a lot of careers since then, and I find them quite fascinating. I often tell young writers what it is and how it is done to build a career in the literary world just in case they want to do it. But it is not something that I have ever personally recommended to myself. There are some very notable writers whose progress has been interesting because of what they've done aside from their writing for their writing. Get yourself a good promo person. A career requires devotion to itself.

The Interviewers

Bruce Meyer was born in 1957 in Toronto and was educated at the University of Toronto, where he received his M.A., and McMaster University where he received his Ph.D. He has served as an Editor with *Descant, Poetry Canada Review*, and co-edited *The Selected Poems of Frank Prewett* (with Barry Callaghan), *Separate Islands: Contemporary British and Irish Poetry* (with Carolyn Meyer), and *Arrivals: Canadian Poetry in the Eighties*. He was a contributor to *The Oxford Companion to Canadian Literature*, and Canadian Advisor and contributor to *Contemporary Poets*. He is co-author with Brian O'Riordan of *In Their Words: Interviews with Fourteen Canadian Writers, Profiles in Canadian Literature: Leonard Cohen*, author of the poetry collections *The Open Room* and *Radio Silence*, and the critical monographs *Profiles in Canadian Literature: Robert Service* and *Profiles in Canadian Literature: Frank Prewett*. He has taught at the University of Toronto, McMaster University, and the University of Windsor, and has held doctoral and post-doctoral fellowships from the Social Sciences and Humanities Research Council of Canada. He lives in Toronto.

Brian O'Riordan was born in Dublin, Ireland, in 1953 and educated at the University of Toronto where he received his M.A. He has served as a Co-Editor of *Descant*. His poems and reviews have appeared in several Canadian magazines and journals. With Bruce Meyer he co-wrote *In Their Words: Interviews with Fourteen Canadian Writers*, and *Profiles in Canadian Literature: Leonard Cohen*. He is currently employed by the Ontario Hospital Association, and is married and lives in Brantford, Ontario.